THE PIRELLI HISTORY OF
MOTOR SPORT

THE PIRELLI HISTORY OF
MOTOR SPORT
L.J.K. SETRIGHT

FREDERICK MULLER LIMITED
LONDON

CONTENTS

	Proem	7
1	AN INFANCY OF TITANS	11
	1894–1920	
2	TIME WILL RUN BACK AND FETCH THE AGE OF GOLD	81
	1921–1934	
3	THE NATIONS RAGE SO FURIOUSLY	123
	1935–1957	
4	THE TOBACCO-FLAVOURED, CANDY-COLOURED, RUBBER-FEATURED SLIDE SHOW	179
	1958–1969	
5	DEVOLUTION	205
	1970–1980	
	ENVOY	221
	Acknowledgements	222
	Index	223

First published in Great Britain 1981 by
Frederick Muller Limited, London NW2 6LE

Copyright © 1981 L. J. K. Setright

Designed by Mike Jarvis

ISBN 0 584 10385 9

Printed in Singapore

Effectively the first organized motor race was from Paris to Rouen in 1894. The prize went to a Daimler-engined Peugeot.

That other motor-car pioneer Benz was also represented; this was a Roger-Benz.

Another prize went to Panhard-Levassor, this one also Daimler-powered; but the fastest of them all was steam-driven.

PROEM

This book was not my idea. For that you may thank Bob Newman of Pirelli, in whose head it must have begun to dawn in 1977 when he noted that seventy years had passed since the Milanese tyremasters had celebrated their first success in motor sport. It was their tyres that had borne the considerable weight of the Itala in which Prince Scipione Borghese won the sensational and supremely difficult Peking to Paris trial.

Now that there is talk of celebrating the 75th anniversary of that event with another motor rally between those same capitals, it can do no harm to recall the 1907 original – not merely because of the historical span that it offers, and certainly not because of its significance in the story of Pirelli's associations with the sport, but because it was conducted in the most sporting spirit, and won by the noblest and most magnanimous of drivers, in the history of competition motoring.

With France the home of motor sport, it was natural and proper that the idea should emanate from the French newspaper *Le Matin*. It seemed natural, too, that Paris should be the destination, for (as we shall see in Chapter 1) all the earliest motoring events of any importance featured the French capital, either as starting or finishing point if not both – and if not, the other extremity was as likely as not to be some foreign capital. The chaotically dangerous days of the great city-to-city races had come to an end in 1903, but none had been as ambitious nor as simple as this. The Great Circle route from Peking to Paris covered about 4925 miles of the earth's circumference, if any crow were fool enough to fly it; but by road the route amounted to more like 8000 miles. Not that much of it was on roads: it took the cars through the mud of mountains and the sludge of paddy-fields, over bridges that were sometimes too weak and sometimes non-existent, across the Gobi desert; and it took the winner two months to complete the trip. He started on 10 June 1907 along with four other smaller French cars, which were all that finally lined up in Peking of the twenty-six entrants, who had each paid 2000 francs for the privilege of risking their lives for a prize so nominal that it was almost derisory – the first bottle from the 1898 vintage of the Moët et Chandon Brut Imperial. The Italian Prince was not fond of gigglewater, as it happened; but it was the conduct of the event rather than its rewards that mattered to him. It was he who negotiated with tribesmen, on behalf of all five contestants, for help in manhandling the cars out of sloughs of mud or seas of sand, across flooding rivers and immuring mountains. He assumed responsibility for the less powerful cars that were contesting the event with him, and would turn back to tow one out of a swamp or to lift another on to railway lines when the parallel road was too rough for it. His 35/45-horsepower Itala, though not cast in the gigantic mould of the 14-litre 120-horsepower Itala racer that won the Coppa Florio at Brescia in that same year, enjoyed such power as was expected of 7·4 litres in those days; but its substance was sometimes its own undoing, for although its Pirelli tyres might bear its considerable weight, at least two river bridges on the Prince's route failed to do so. All these adversities were faced in the same spirit, and only when he had shepherded his rivals as far as was necessary for them to be reasonably sure of completing the course (which they all did) did he allow his chauffeur Ettore Guizzardi to give the Itala its head, arriving outside the offices of *Le Matin* in Paris on 10 August, three weeks ahead of the field.

That, albeit all too rarely, is what motor sport can bring out in a man, always provided that he have it in him. However, competition is not always a matter of transcontinental ethics; there may be as much sportsmanship *pro rata* among today's fraternity of drag-racers, sprinting over a mere 440 yards – and in some other branches of motoring competition there may appear to be none whatsoever, an unblushingly commercial fame applying the spur instead. There is nothing new in this; as much could be said in 1907, or even earlier; but however euphemistic the expression occasionally seems (and the word *occasionally* should be stressed), motor sport flourishes today as never before, even though the degree of variegation is no greater than it always was, right from its very beginnings. That is why this book is intended to map with pictures and trace the words not only the mainstreams but also some of the backwaters, to plot the courses of history and geography, of amateurism and professionalism and nationalism, of technical evolution and commercial devolution, and all the changes and continuities that have made motor sport the epitome of *plus ca change, plus c'est la même chose.*

As I have said, the existence of the book is due to Bob Newman; but that was by no means his only good idea. He deserves no less praise for his choice of that gifted historian L. J. K. Setright to write it. On this author must be laid the blame for the kind of book that it is, and the gratitude for the kind of book that it is not, which is a matter of much greater import. It is not meant to be an exhaustive or exhausting treatise, one of those books of encyclopaedic detail, narrative complexity and inenarrable boredom. This author and numerous others have written far too many of that kind already. Thus the reader may be invited to dip a tentative toe into technicalities, but should not be required to wade through a foam of engineering. The progress of technology may seem vitally important when measured from year to year or even from decade to decade; but when seen across the span of a history that began in 1894, the metallic skeleton of competitive motoring looks better when adorned with human flesh. The opportunity to see this is one of the benisons of history's liberal spectrum; you would never enjoy such vision in the monochromatic light of science.

Consider for example those beautiful Alfa Romeos which dominated the Grands Prix from 1946 to 1951. What really remains in the memory is that they were beautiful. You may learn elsewhere from that distinguished analyst L. J. K. Setright that in their final 1951 form they reached an unprecedented 4800 ft/minimum mean piston speed while attaining a brake mean effective pressure of 338 pounds per square inch, under the influence of two-stage boosting beyond two atmospheres, and with the assistance of needle-roller big-end bearings. The very meanness of brake mean effective pressure should indicate to us its relative importance: what really mattered was that these cars looked blood-red, sounded like Jove's trumpets, went like the devil, and smelled of brown paper and boot polish. What mattered no less was that they were driven (and could be seen to be driven) by men of such calibre as the impeccably stylish Dr. Giuseppe Farina, the uncannily positive Juan Manuel Fangio, and the sturdily human Luigi Fagioli. They were, after all, not demi-gods; yet it was enough, that reality of flesh and blood. The factory told us that the 1951 Alfa Romeo racer rendered 404 brake horsepower, and we were quite content to believe them, even had the truth been nearer 202 – for they were synthetic horsepower, not to be confused with the inimitable realities of flesh and blood. After all, in the Paris-Trouville race of 1899, when a handicap equated four racing cars (the fastest was a Mors) with motorcycles, pedal cycles, horses and pedestrians, it was a horse that won.

Pallida Mors aequo pulsat . . .

To drag in both horse and Horace, and to wring such inferences out of a trivial historical fact, might seem such desperate measures as might only be essayed by that prize idiot L. J. K. Setright; but another of the attractions of history is that it is illuminated by its trivia. A painstaking account of the 100-horsepower Panhard racer would provide a less telling commentary on the times than an account of the rare incident involving the Chevalier de Knyff when driving that car over the course of the 1905 Gordon Bennett race: swerving to avoid a peasant woman who had run into the road in pursuit of an errant cow, he was left with no option but to smite that unfortunate beast with the Panhard, destroying them both – and he observed later from his sick bed, as he recovered from his own injuries: *If you have to hit something, choose a cow; they are so soft.*

Greater men have uttered greater idiocies. Consider Henry Ford, who so contemptuously dismissed history as bunk: he was no less peevish and petulant in dismissing the new six-cylinder car introduced by his rival Chevrolet with the words: *I've got no use for a car that has more spark plugs than a cow has teats.* He would not let it be known at the time, but he had been working on a five-cylinder engine himself, a project which demanded more engineering expertise than he could muster. Either he was too shy to look at a cow full in the udder, or else he could not count.

What is one to make of such a figure as Henry Ford, the only man to design and build a record-breaking car with an unsprung chassis? Not too little – for he was brave enough to drive the car, and he got his record, at 91·37 mph over an all too literally flying mile on the ice of Lake St. Clair. Flesh and blood, courage and cussedness, count for as much in our history as steel and rubber; nor can we discount hedges or ditches, timber or masonry, board tracks or concrete, macadam or dust. That is why this is principally a picture book, intended to make the most of photographs and artwork which reflect the tastes and techniques of the times under review, illustrating not only the central theme of the sport, but also the peripheral context of social, political, economic and ecumenical growth. The text will, with any luck, provide a linking commentary that should perform the same functions. Part of my ambitions for the book was that each chapter should be distinguished according to the styles fashionable during the period it covered, and that its language should reflect contemporary usages either in journalism or belles-lettres. This may be traced in some decay of formality, from the era of Chapter 1 when a gentleman driver was a Mr. Jarrott, if not the Baron de Caters or Count Masetti, to the times of Chapter 4 when Clark would be Jimmy and Stewart Jackie. However, the effect may penetrate deeper than that: and if the sensitive reader should shudder at some echo of such famous writers as P. G. Widehouse, Edith Satwell, Louise MacNice, Ramon Dunyan and Tam Wolfe, or the infamous motorcycling author Long John Kick-Start, I would not be at all surprised.

L.J.K.S. – Suburbiton 1981

CHAPTER ONE

AN INFANCY OF TITANS

1894–1920

There were giants in the earth in those days – and many emerged in the great inter-city races of the pioneers. Hillclimbs offered the other extreme, but gradually the sport stratified. The Grands Prix promoted the racing car, the Prince Heinrich trials gave birth to the sports car, the Tourist Trophy (so it was fondly hoped) to the tourer; the Gordon Bennett races fostered nationalism, and the Great War intervened to show what nationalism could do. Before it started, the giants were giving way to voiturettes: brute force took refuge in Brooklands, bloody ignorance at Indianapolis. After it had finished, the motor vehicle meant much more to many more people.

Man cannot help being an idealist. Because of this he loves and prays and fights and writes and does all manner of irrational things; but the situation is made more complicated by the fact that all men do not share the same ideals. Because of that, each man will insist by sermon and sword that his personal ideals are the truest; and so to confirm the excellence of his own judgement, whether to impress others or for his own peace of mind, he will demand recognition that his lady is the loveliest, his god the greatest, his fist the hardest and his car the fastest. Thus the pursuit of his ideals makes him as ready to compete as to collaborate; and thus it is not the fault of historians but rather the fault of mankind that we cannot state for certainty when the first motor race took place, but must instead assume that it was when two motorists first met on the same stretch of road.

Whatever the occasion and outcome of any such informal encounter, we have a clearer notion of the first organized motoring competition. In 1887 a French journal, *Le Vélocipède*, attempted to arrange a sort of trial, though it was unlikely to amount to anything much more strenuous than a short run out into the country, starting in the outskirts of Paris; since only one competitor turned up, the event was a nullity. In 1894, however, the newspaper *Le Petit Journal* was more successful in organizing a competitive run – a trial rather than a race – over a 79-mile route from Paris to Rouen. This attracted an amazing variety of entries: a baricycle moved by the weight of passengers, and others propelled by 'a combination of animate and mechanical motor' or 'a multiple system of levers' or dismissed as simply 'automatic', were included in the 102 machines entered when the lists closed on 30 April. When the competitors were marshalled for the start on 22 July there were only twenty-one of them, and they were all propelled either by steam or by petrol. It was a steamer that finished first, a De Dion tractor which averaged 11.6 mph and therefore needed little more than half of the twelve hours that were allowed for the journey – but it also needed the attention of

The citizens of Mantes are variously interested or indifferent, but not yet terrified, by the passage of participants in the Paris-Rouen run. It is 1894, and the racing has not yet started . . .

13

The purposeful attitude of a driver summoning as much as five horsepower to propel his Roger-Benz phaeton in the 1895 Paris-Bordeaux-Paris race prompts apprehension in the onlookers, though the pedal cyclist riding in pursuit seems not at all extended. Some gentlemen stood forward quite boldly, however, at the Versailles start as M. Emile Levassor (below) set off on his epic drive.

two crewmen, and so its driver the Marquis de Dion was not allowed to receive the first prize. It went instead to Peugeot and Panhard.

Those two manufacturers had not dead-heated; the inconclusive nature of the result was due to the regulations officially ignoring average speeds provided that they were within the permitted range. Motorists' appetites were whetted, however, and it was felt that something faster and more strenuous was called for, a proper race in fact. The Marquis de Dion and the Baron de Zuylen de Nyevelt took themselves off to Pierre Giffard, editor of *Le Petit Journal*, calling on him to sponsor a full-scale race over a distance of as much as 700 miles. The paper's proprietors were aghast: *No one could complain at a competition in which reliability was the chief factor; but a long race in which speed was the be-all and end-all is quite another thing. Supposing an accident were to take place – and if these automobiles could really attain the terrifying speed of fifteen or twenty miles an hour on the ordinary road, as had been proved in the Paris-Rouen trial, such a catastrophe was more than likely to happen – it would offer an opportunity to the political opponents of* Le Petit Journal *which they could exploit to disastrous effect.*

The Marquis and the Baron were not to be put off: they wanted their race and they convened a committee to organize it. From that committee grew the Automobile Club of France, destined to be for a long time the most important sanctioning body in the sport; but the committee's immediate offspring was a race over 732 miles from Paris to Bordeaux and back, to be held in the summer of 1895. Criticism was anticipated: sheer speed was not being encouraged, they said, but a combination of speed and reliability, for cars which were merely fast could not win if they broke down. Any car with only two seats was obviously designed for speed (a modern insurance industry would be proud of such prejudice!) and so could not be eligible for the main prize: four-seaters were *de rigueur*.

Nevertheless it was a two-seater that put up by far the best performance, one that signalled the emergence of a pair of names that were to dominate racing for some years to come, Panhard et Levassor. Driving through the night behind a miserable pair of oil-lamps, Emile Levassor reached Bordeaux three hours ahead of the field, supped on either champagne or soup (the authorities are at variance) and drove back to extend his lead by a further three and a half hours, his two-seater Panhard averaging 15 mph to complete the trip in just over two days. The prizewinner, the first four-seater, was a Peugeot that finished third overall in nearly sixty hours, and the last of the nine finishers was an old Bollée steamer which averaged a mere 6 mph. At least it finished; thirteen did not, including a Peugeot driven by André Michelin who had the temerity to run it on pneumatic tyres.

By the end of that same year the ACF, the Automobile Club de France, had been formed, and was

Storms en route, flowers at the finish: M. Merkel's 6hp Panhard, second in the Paris-Marseilles race of 1896.

planning its first race for 1896. This was over 1063 miles from Paris to Marseilles and back, and was expected to take ten days. Breaking the journey into daily stages was meant to avoid straining the drivers – in those pioneer days people were concerned with the performance of the machines, not that of the men – but the drivers were doomed to have a terrible time. On the second day a freak storm blew up, with winds so strong that they could stop a car head-on, or blow it off the road when on the beam. Trees and telegraph poles were uprooted, roads became quagmires, and accidents were numerous. Levassor's Panhard capsized after hitting a dog, giving the man internal injuries from which he was to die in the following year. Two other Panhards collided with carts; a Bollée and a Rochet-Schneider were savaged by furious bulls. Only fourteen of the twenty-three starters got back to Paris, and the first three were all Panhards.

By 1897 it was evidently no longer obligatory for motor races to start from Paris, although a couple of minor events (to Dieppe and to Trouville) did. In Germany, which was after all where the motor car came from originally, they organized their first competition as a trial from Berlin to Potsdam, and this was to pave the way for later races from Berlin to Leipzig and from Frankfurt to Köln. Years later, in 1908 when

Racing wear was less stereotyped than facial hair in 1896.

everybody else had given up city-to-city races, there was even a frightful affair that ran from St. Petersburg to Moscow: it was won by Hémery driving a Benz at an average speed of 51·4 mph for the 438 miles. Around the turn of the century however, Paris was still The Place – or at least France, which although unable to claim parentage of the petrol-engined car, was undoubtedly the nursery of motoring and of motor sport. The same was true in aviation: the powered heavier-than-air craft may have been born in America, but it was nurtured in France.

It was a social phenomenon. The motorists of the *fin de siècle* were invariably well-to-do and frequently well connected, and France was the hub of polite society. Fashionable holidaymakers flocked to the Riviera for the winter season, and so it was there in January 1897 that the major event of the year took place, over a fairly short but arduous route from Marseilles via Nice to La Turbie. Society, which may not have exercised its mind over the finer points of internal combustion, doubtless took pleasure in the victory of the Comte de Chasseloup-Laubat driving a De Dion steamer.

If the interest of society was superficial, that of the fraternity of motoring enthusiasts became fanatical.

The great Paris race of 1898, the first to cross an international frontier – it ran over 889 miles to Amsterdam and back – saw the first cars built specifically for racing. There was also for the first time a separate class for light cars weighing no more than 400 kg, and another for tourers. Speeds were rising, standards growing more severe, and still Panhard reigned supreme; and this remained true in the following year when the ACF set a circular route of 1350 miles passing through the mountains of the Auvergne for their Tour de France. It was won at 30·2 mph by the Chevalier René de Knyff, portly and popular, a very safe driver and a director of Panhard. His was to prove one of the most distinguished of motor-sporting careers: he had scored his first victory in the Paris-Bordeaux-Paris race of 1898 after finishing fourth in his first event, the Marseilles-Nice-La Turbie race of 1897, and he was to become the most successful of the pioneer racing men before devoting himself to the organizational side of the sport, retiring from the presidency of the CSI (the Commission Sportive Internationale) in 1946.

There was very nearly no racing for him or for anybody else in 1900, when – albeit for less than a month – there was a total ban on racing in France. This had been triggered by an accident involving spectators in a race for tricycles, but it heightened a certain antipathy for motoring in general and racing in particular that was beginning to make itself felt, even in France, as it had always in England and Switzerland. There had been some evidence of this as early as the Paris-Amsterdam-Paris race of 1898, although it took such a farcical turn that the comedy overshadowed the controversy. What happened was that one Monsieur Bochet, who was examining engineer to the Prefect of Police of Paris, took it on himself to insist that all the cars should be certified as roadworthy according to an obsolete but unrepealed law. Since no entrant could furnish the appropriate certificate, Monsieur Bochet himself examined and failed most of the cars, and refused permission for the race to begin. Lest anyone defy his authority, he posted a squadron of infantry on the Joinville road, set up a couple of guns on the Bry road, and took a half squadron of the 23rd Hussars to the official starting point for the race, assuring any potential dissident of summary obliteration. The organizers did not defy Monsieur Bochet; they simply moved the start to a neighbouring département that was outside his jurisdiction.

It was a straw in the wind, however. Fanatics are generally unpopular, fanatical drivers no less than others; and the 1901 Paris-Berlin race, in which 110 cars started, was described by contemporaries as 'the race of madmen'. Every village along the 687-mile route had received a warning of the dangers of speeding cars, but it was impossible for the whole route to be policed; and there was just one fatal accident, when a small boy was run over near Reims.

Voiture sportive, *1900*

Because of the disapproval engendered by this accident, there was only one Paris race in 1902, but it was the biggest yet, with 118 cars setting off for Vienna and taking in the 5000 ft Arlberg Pass on the way. The results were surprising: a car constructed by Monsieur Louis Renault and driven by his brother Marcel in the category for light cars up to 650 kg (heavy cars were allowed 1000 kg while those below 400 were classed as voiturettes) was fastest of all, with another light car, a Darracq, splitting the heavyweight Panhard of Monsieur Henri Farman (later famous as a pioneer aviator) and the Mercédès of the celebrated racing driver, Count Eliot Zborowski. Here was another straw in the wind for those who had missed the showing of Louis Renault's voiturettes which had finished eighth overall in the Paris-Berlin race: the giants of the road (the 1901 Mors weighed nearly 2900 lb, could do more than 75 mph, and had very little in the way of brakes) were outgrowing themselves, and the more agile lightweights were beginning to cut them down to size. A popular criticism of heavy cars of this period, and especially those racing subject to a

Voiture de course, *1901*
In fact the supreme racing car of 1901 was the Mors.
Mercédès served notice to the French makers that their
opposition was growing stronger, by winning the Nice-
Salon-Nice race early in the season; but in the 60hp 10.1-
litre Mors seen opposite, M. Henri Fournier was able to
score a magnificent double victory later in the year. He won
the race from Paris to Bordeaux at more than 53 mph, and
at over 44 mph he took the laurels in the greatest race yet,
the 'race of madmen' from Paris to Berlin.

maximum weight limit of 1000 kg, was that they were rendered dangerous by the lightening of their chassis to accept vast and necessarily very heavy engines. This case has perhaps been overstated, for those engines were not necessarily so heavy. Piston displacement is after all a matter of cavities, which weigh nothing, and if the skill of the designer be such that they can be contained by thin-walled cylinders and supporting structures, then an engine of inordinate capacity might nevertheless have quite moderate mass. Despite a sump like a bathtub and pistons like stewpans, a representative 1-ton racer's engine would in those days weigh less than 700 lb, representing an engine: vehicle weight ratio not very different from that of a modern racing car.

Be that as it may, such cars were popularly deemed dangerous. Certainly the spectating crowds had little concept of the difficulties the drivers faced in controlling their machines on exiguous tyres and execrable roads; and in the 1903 Paris-Madrid race, held despite the disapproval of the French government, this combination of speed, dust and massed humanity proved fatal.

Everything had been done to encourage spectators: the race was being started at 3.30 a.m. on a May Sunday so that as many people as possible could watch, and the crowd pouring out of Paris to watch the start from Versailles was estimated at 100,000. They lined the route with Chinese lanterns, they crowded on to the roads for a better view, and they filled the drivers with a dangerous mixture of fear and fury. The difficulties were described by the first of the 179 drivers to set off, the Englishman Mr. Charles Jarrott, as upright and sporting a gentleman as ever became a founder of the Automobile Association or a lieutenant colonel. A driver of immense experience, great enterprise and considerable success, he was leader of the De Dietrich team in this event, and was to be credited with third place when it finished prematurely a few hours later. At the very beginning he was aware of impending doom: *It seemed impossible that my swaying bounding car could miss the reckless spectators. A wedge-shaped space opened out in the crowd as I approached, and so fine was the calculation made that at times it seemed impossible for the car not to overtake the apex of the human triangle and deal death and destruction. I tried slowing down, but quickly realized that the danger was as great at 40 miles an hour as at 80. It merely meant that the crowd waited a longer time in the road; and the remembrance of those hundreds of cars behind me* (these events were run as time trials against the clock, the cars starting at regular intervals of about a minute and being timed individually), *the realization that the hunt had commenced, made me put on top speed, and hope that Providence would be kind to the weak intellects which allowed their possessors to run such risks so callously.*

As he feared, there were dreadful accidents. The day was hot, the roads dreadfully dusty, the crowd as thick on the ground as between the ears. In the clouds of dust, the drivers sped on unable to see. Others fell

Seven hours faster than the Arlberg Express, M. Marcel Renault covered the Paris-Vienna course so fast that he arrived at the finish before the officials. In the tragic Paris-Madrid event, the lightweight Renault which arrived first at the Bordeaux checkpoint above was driven by the designer M. Louis Renault.

foul of level crossing gates closed and deserted by the signalmen. Numerous oxen were killed and dogs too, one of the latter jamming the steering of a De Dietrich which then ran head first at 80 mph into a tree. Cars collided with each other, smashed into walls, rolled into ditches. Marcel Renault overturned, to die later from his injuries, Stead was similarly crushed, Porter's mechanic wiped off and burned against a wall. Tourand's mechanic was killed when the car went into the crowd: Tourand wrenched at the wheel of his Brouhot trying to dodge a soldier who had dashed after a child that had run into the road – and the soldier and the child were killed too. Several spectators lost their lives as well as at least five drivers and mechanics; and the whole of France was in an uproar over what became known as the Race of Death. The government had to step in, and the race was halted at Bordeaux. The cars were not even allowed to return under their own power, but were ignominiously towed by horses to the railway station and put on a train for Paris. The leading driver at Bordeaux was the intrepid but elsewhere unsuccessful Monsieur Fernand Gabriel, who

The light and agile Renault redirected the thoughts of other designers in the early years of the century. Number three, in these pages, was driven by M. Louis Renault himself in the fateful 1903 Paris-Madrid race. Wearing a Coke (or, as the undiscriminating will have it, a Bowler) hat, he attends the weighing-in; protected by a dust-helmet, he took the lead before Chartres and never relinquished it.

Pedal cyclists escorted racing cars through the towns, acting as marshals in the Paris-Madrid race. Cycling experience prompted Renault to fit nail-catchers behind the rear tyres of his racers. The cars weighed only 1200 lb, and were brilliantly competitive but not overpowered with 40-brake horsepower; but if their speed was not too much for them, the conditions were. One of the most lamented losses was of the driver of car number 63, the proprietor's brother M. Marcel Renault, the commercial and administrative brain of the firm. Blinded by the dust, he spun off at a bend near Couhé-Vèrac and died without regaining consciousness. His mechanic Vauthier was seriously injured.

started 168th but urged his Mors through all the dust and cars and carnage to average 65·3 mph. Second, and shocked to learn after his arrival that his brother had crashed, was Louis Renault in a light car of his own make.

But nobody cared who won; they only grieved for those lost. Racing on open roads had been doomed for some time, and from now on it was dead. The Paris-Madrid was the last of the classic city-to-city races (the Peking to Paris affair of 1907 was cast in a very different mould) and although other forms of racing would be formed to succeed them, motor racing would never be quite the same again. The only consolation to be sought in the disaster was expressed by Mr. Jarrott: *To my mind, it was a fitting end to an inevitable happening, that the curtain should have been run down on the Paris to Bordeaux road, the scene of many a titanic struggle and the road on which Levassor himself showed to the world at large, in the first great motor race in history, the vast and far-reaching possibilities of the motor propelled vehicle.*

Those possibilities had greatly impressed Mr. James Gordon Bennett, the expatriate son of the eponymous founder and publisher of the New York Herald. He indulged his great enthusiasm for sports, devoting a good deal of his time to acquiring expertise as boxer, swimmer and ball-player, while yet managing his business interests well enough for him to be able to draw more than a million dollars a year for more than forty years. Combining his newspaperman's taste for sensationalism with his dilettante interest in sport, it came naturally that he should take an interest in motor racing; and in 1899 he put up a cup bearing his name, to be won in an annual race that was meant to be of major importance. The technical specifications of the cars involved were those which prevailed for the time being in racing formally for the *Grande Voiture* – an expression which a Buddhist might construe as the big vehicle, the British taxation authorities as the heavy motorcar. What was much more significant to the regulation of the races for the Gordon Bennett cup was the set of rules governing the nationality of the entrants. The cup was not to be contested by drivers nor by factories but in effect by nations, each country's recognized national club having the right to nominate a team of three cars, every part of which had to be made in the country which it represented. National racing colours were also stipulated, and the responsibility for organizing the race and acting as hosts to the competitors was laid upon the last club to win the race; for the first event, the Automobile Club of France was naturally accorded that honour.

They responded to that compliment by fielding a team of three cars for the 1900 event; but nobody else took much notice, the host country's only rivals being a solitary Belgian and an equally lone American car. In the following year the French team were the only starters, a Napier having been disqualified because its

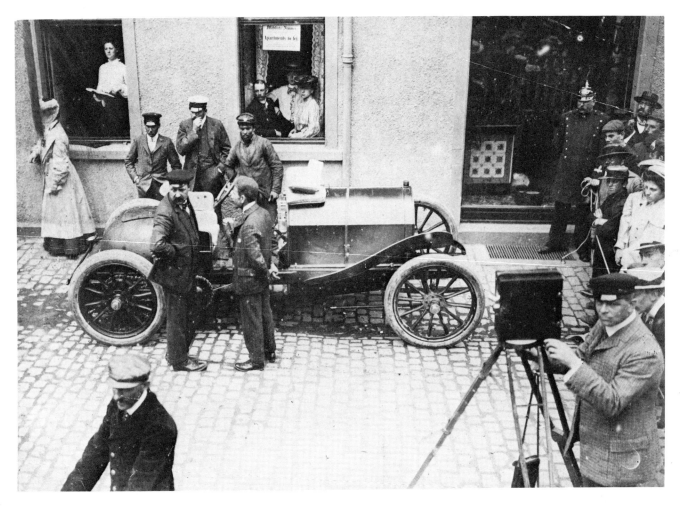

Photographers and society
flocked in the wake of the
Kaiser himself to see the
Mercédès win the 1904
Gorden Bennett Trophy;
but neither they nor the
Fiat team (below) led by
Sig. Lancia, could match
the virtuosity of 'le
chronometre', M. Leon
Théry, in the French
Richard-Brasier.

GORDON·BENNETT·RENNEN
The Gordon·Bennett·Cup   La Coupe Gordon·Bennett

Lancia auf Fiat

Cagno auf Fiat   Jtalienische Fahrer   Storero auf Fiat

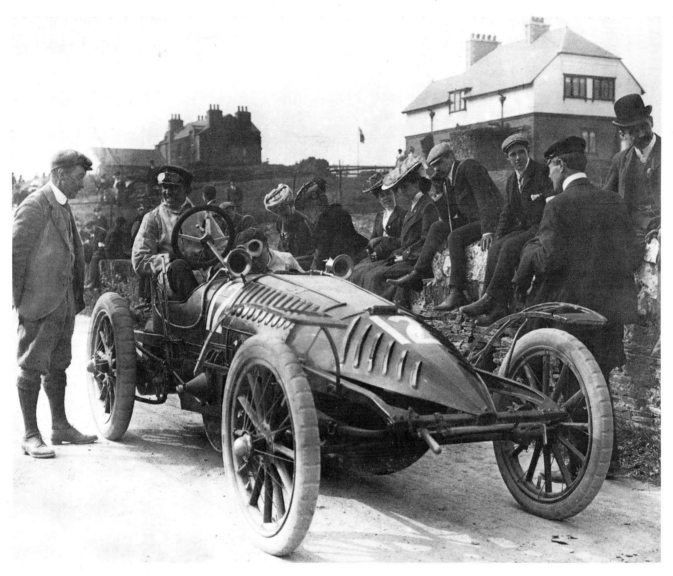

Mr. Charles Jarrott at the wheel of the Wolseley 'Beetle' in the Isle of Man trials for the 1904 Gordon Bennett race.

tyres were not made in Britain; and since the race was to be run on French territory, a Panhard having won the 1900 event, the Gordon Bennett affair was run off as part of the Paris to Bordeaux race. Much the same happened in 1902, the accommodation being found in the Paris to Vienna event. This time the British challenge succeeded, and Mr. S. F. Edge brought back with his victorious Napier the responsibility for organizing the 1903 race.

Parliament would not hear of it. Racing motorcars on the public highway was viewed as heresy by this horsedrawn society, and eventually the Royal Automobile Club was fobbed off with a closed circuit on roads at Athy in Ireland where, presumably, it was assumed that heresy might pass unnoticed. Closed-circuit races had been run before, but none of such importance; and since all subsequent races for the Gordon Bennett Cup were similarly staged, the series could be said to have confirmed this usage beginning as it did in the year when the unhappy Paris-Madrid event was recognized as the last of the city-to-city races. In a little while the Gordon Bennett races would be succeeded by the Grands Prix. These were to assume

Motor racing inspired New and Old World artisans and aristocrats alike. Mercédès driver H. Wilhelm Pöge (top left) offers visible contrast to another, Lautenschlager (bottom left). Hawk-nosed M. Camille Jenatzy has the lineage of a Belgian gentleman: stogey-faced Barney Oldfield is emphatically American.

immediately and to retain permanently the status of the highest form of motor racing; yet it was the Gordon Bennett races which set the style.

Style was clearly important, at a time when motoring was still of practical interest only to the wealthy. It evidently mattered particularly to the Germans, for while America merely sent a couple of assorted cars and the French a mixed threesome, with the British industry offering so many different entrants that eliminating trials had to be held, the Automobil Club von Deutschland entered a team of three matched Mercédès 90-horsepower racing cars. The organization of this team, furnished by the German Daimler company, was entrusted to that distinguished gentleman Emil Jellinek, who had encouraged Daimler's gifted engineer

An advanced American, the Packard 'Gray Wolf', fourth in the 1904 Vanderbilt Cup race.

Maybach in the creation of the first modern motor car, the 1901 model which Jellinek dubbed with the name of his elder daughter Mercédès. The diplomatic Jellinek moved in the highest circles, but there were those who considered him capable of unfortunate lapses of taste: the German club did not approve of his choice of drivers. Perhaps because of his rabbinical parentage or because of his adventurous early life in South America, he seemed less snobbish than his peers; or perhaps, after a brief competition career driving Daimlers on such occasions as the Nice Speed Week (comprizing a race of sorts, a sprint along the Promenade des Anglais and a hillclimb at La Turbie) he had concluded that such dirty and dangerous work was not for the fastidious but better delegated to hired menials. At any rate he nominated Werner and

Driving a 75hp Fiat alongside the railway, Sig. Vincenzo Lancia in the 1904 race from Brescia via Cremona and Mantua back to Brescia.

Hieronymus as Mercédès drivers; but the German Automobile Club, acting on social grounds, refused them permission to compete. The honour of Germany could only be represented by gentlemen who were *hochwohlgeborene* (of high birth) – and by some curious process of elimination, this meant that Germany's honour had to be upheld by two Belgians, the Baron Pierre de Caters and Camille Jenatzy, and the Englishman Mr. Foxhall Keene.

Germany's representation had to be adjusted afresh when a fire at the Daimler factory destroyed the three big racers that had been purpose-built for the Gordon Bennett. A trio of 60-horsepower tourers was borrowed back from customers and was hastily fitted with racing bodywork and painted white for the occasion, for this year the rules about national racing colours were to be enforced. This was indeed the occasion on which the colour sometimes called British Racing Green first appeared, but in strict truth there is no such colour, and never has been: the paint so proudly worn by Bentleys, MGs and Aston Martins in years to come was, ironically, Parson's Napier Green.

To judge from the way that he drove, Jenatzy probably only saw red. That was the colour of his beard, and he was even nicknamed Le Diable Rouge (the red devil) mainly on account of a driving style that was, to say the least, exuberant, having been developed since he began his competition career in 1898 – to become, within months, holder of the world speed record and the first man to drive at more than 100 kilometres per hour, which he did in his own electric aerodyne La Jamais Contente. He himself may have been briefly content after the 1903 Gordon Bennett race, for he won it by nearly twelve minutes and brought the cup back to Germany; but there the following year he had to be content with second place, being like all the others put in the shade by the spectacular performance of the Frenchman Leon Théry in a mighty Richard-Brasier. One can imagine the spectating Kaiser Wilhelm II and his Kaiserin feeling somewhat discontented at this turn of events too, for the Germans had done everything possible to hedge their bets for this race on their home territory in the Taunus. Taking advantage of the regulations about construction in the country of the entrant club, they arranged for a duplicate set of Mercédès racers to be built in Austria. Even without these supernumeraries it would have been a good field, with entries from Italy, Belgium, and Switzerland, as well as France. It did not matter; regardless of their numbers Monsieur Théry was invincible. He repeated his performance the following year at Clermont-Ferrand against an unprecedented field of eighteen cars from six countries including the USA. This was more than the French liked: they had plenty of willing representatives, but the rules allowed them only three. It meant holding eliminating trials; but there was no difficulty in turning them to good purpose, and as this contemporary extract reveals, it was quite an occasion.

A cannon-shot, a trumpet-call: in a deafening hub-bub like a volley of musket-fire, a car passes like a tornado, dancing over the irregularities of the road-surface, between the two rows of grandstands . . . In the formidable thunder of his four cylinders, simultaneously leaping and skidding over the road, Théry's car crosses the finishing line. Arms and hats are waved, cheers ring out . . . Between two hedges of gendarmes and soldiers, Théry enters the paddock . . . He leaps from his car to fall into the arms of Brasier. They embrace: Théry's chubby face, all black with dust, grease and Pulveranto road dressing, presses on the pale cheek of Brasier. And Théry demands something to drink . . .

This doughty pilot repeated his success in the event proper, driving that same gargantuan Richard-Brasier of 11·3 litres. Since 1902, the cars had been restricted to a maximum weight of 1000 kilogrammes, and many were the allegations of excessive power being accommodated at the expense of structural weakness. Whether that be true or not – and it is probably true of the earliest cars, whose wooden chassis were merely strengthened locally by flitch plates – racing cars of this ilk and those built for the subsequent international Grand Prix went, until at least 1911, through a monstrous infancy. The most effective machines had engines ranging in displacement from about 8 litres to more than 18, and were built with such generosity of metal as was judged appropriate to races that might endure for two days over roads that were poor to begin with and would deteriorate rapidly as the mighty cars passed.

Not all motor racing was of such heroic scale. There were even some competitions that occupied mere minutes, and might extend over a course only a few kilometres long. In England indeed they might be shorter still, measurable in hundreds of yards – but every yard would be significant, every tenth of a second

that could be won by the perfect negotiation of a painfully tight corner would be critical. These were the hillclimbs, in which cars did not race each other, but ran one at a time against the clock. This is a peculiarly difficult and peculiarly satisfying form of the sport, for each driver can know none of the spur of physical competition, enjoy none of the company of rivals on the track with him to give guidance as to the pace required to beat them. All he can do is his best, and hope that it is better than the best of his opponents. Hillclimbs are hard; they could also in the early days be humdrum, for their history began when merely to be able to climb a given hill would suffice to win honours. In time their pace was to become so furious, and their demands so specialized, that only the best of Grand Prix drivers could occasionally dare to compete in them; but they had never enjoyed the glamour of some other forms of racing, and because of their deliberately awkward locations they could never attract such crowds. What they did do, which was no less important, was to foster a sporting spirit of unrivalled purity and, by avoiding the worst corruptions of commercial sponsorship, to enjoy exceptional longevity. On the mainland of Europe the first hillclimb at Semmering was little more than a club run in 1899, but by 1902 it was a full-blooded speed event, as by that time were certain other ascents including the hillclimb at La Turbie which was such a feature of the Nice Speed Week. In Britain, the thousand-yard climb up what had been a Worcestershire bridle-path at Shelsley Walsh was instituted in 1905 and has continued ever since over the same route, to endure as the oldest surviving motoring competition in the world to maintain a continuity broken only by the Great War and the World War. In America too, hillclimbing attracted its own devotees: the 12·4-mile dirt road that climbs the sides of the 14,110 ft Pikes Peak in the Rocky Mountains of Colorado has seen the dust of its 154 corners disturbed by dicers since 1916. Pikes Peak is in fact an event with an uncanny history of family participation: the Unser family, father, uncle and sons, have won half of the events in the hill's history. To see one of the senior members of the family hurtling uphill into the clouds must be to have a new concept of *Vater Unser in Himmelreich* . . . and if the hill itself did not put the fear of God into you, any of the competing cars almost certainly would.

There are many who were quite dismayed at the development of the racing car in the early years of the century. Things had already progressed a fair way since the pioneer Karl Benz had declared in the 1890s that 'A car which can attain a speed of more than 60 kilometres per hour will soon rattle itself to pieces'; by the time of the Paris Salon of 1902, King Leopold of Belgium was telling Maybach that he needed a car that was faster than anything else on the road. 'Unless I can touch 130 kilometres per hour, it is of no use to me'. Maybach expressed confidence in his company's ability to make anything, and that is how he came to design

the 90-horsepower Mercédès. To many people the 90 was a racer; but in those days a racing car was little more than a touring car with an uncommonly large engine and an uncomfortably stripped body. The spur of competition was changing this, and more and more the racing car was becoming a specialized machine that was fit for nothing else, a deplorable irrelevance in the eyes of those who saw the value of competition as improving the design – and above all the reliability – of the everyday touring car.

This feeling was particularly strong in Britain, where racing on the public highway was forbidden and where the sporting motorist risked ostracism. So it came about that in 1905, the year of the last Gordon Bennett and the first Shelsley Walsh hillclimb, something more conscientiously constructed was proposed by the Royal Automobile Club in the form of the first race for the Tourist Trophy. They had a course available for it in the Isle of Man, that most sturdily self-willed of the British Isles, where the oldest of parliaments had been quite happy to close 52 miles of roads for the 1904 Gordon Bennett eliminating trials. The Tourist Trophy as originally conceived was an event for full touring-bodied cars, ballasted to the equivalent of four adult passengers, with a strict weight limit and a secretly prepared fuel-consumption handicap; and duplicate cars had to be available for sale. The regulations were indeed as challenging as the course itself, which took in the hillclimb of Snaefell; the object was to prove the car's reliability and frugality as much as its roadworthiness and speed. Higher standards were undoubtedly necessary: the poor roads, the mediocre fuels and lubricants, the lackadaisical metallurgy and crude workshop practice all combined to make the mechanical reliability of nearly all cars a matter more of statistical probability than of design excellence.

Most of all, the abysmal incompetence of most drivers made it necessary for a car to withstand monstrous atrocities of mechanical cruelty. As the first TT was to show, this human fallibility could undermine the most exceptional mechanical ability. Such mechanical excellence was just becoming a reality, thanks to the work of Mr. Frederick Henry Royce. He was an engineer of coarse vocabulary and unkempt appearance who had risen from an impoverished childhood to become an electrical engineer of distinction, and principal partner in F. H. Royce & Co. Ltd. of Manchester. Originally that firm had occupied a backyard workshop making domestic bell sets, but had earned a worldwide reputation as manufacturers of electric cranes and dynamos. Mr. Royce had begun to take an interest in motoring in 1902, building his own car a couple of years later, and so sweet were its manners that no less a personage than the Hon. Charles S. Rolls begged to be associated with Royce's business. An enthusiastic sportsman (he was a pioneer aviator as well as a keen racing motorist, and it was flying that was to kill him a few years later), Mr. Rolls was one of the

drivers in the Rolls-Royce team entered for the first TT in 1905.

The preparation of the two cars caused Mr. Royce few headaches. He had already developed nickel steels for his axles and chassis, making it possible to build the cars considerably lighter than with the lower strength materials used by rivals. The advanced design of his carburettor, and the low mechanical losses consequent on the careful manufacture and assembly of the whole car, made the Rolls-Royce naturally frugal. The TT version, copiously lightened with holes in the chassis frame and hubs, with wire-spoked wheels and somewhat filleted coachwork, was a superb car by the standards of its day, and Mr. Rolls soon showed in practice that it was the equal of anything else in the competition. Alas, his excitement got the better of him in the very first lap of the race, and he wrecked the gearbox before he had travelled a mile. Driver Northey in the second Rolls-Royce put in the fastest lap of the day, and finished a close second to the winning Arrol-Johnston. A year later Rolls and the Royce won the TT, and from that point the firm never looked back – nor did it ever go racing again, though it was to take part in several long-distance touring trials, including the Austrian Alpine Trials.

Mrs W.K. Vanderbilt and her daughter led 250,000 spectators to Long Island to see the 1906 Vanderbilt Cup race, in conditions typefied by the lower picture opposite. Above it is the Rolls-Royce winning the 1906 TT; beneath the ladies is burly Otto Salzer, already a professional driver for Mercédès then, and destined to remain one well into the 1920s.

These last were the natural successors to a series of events held in Germany and Austria and conceived in very much the same spirit as the Tourist Trophy. The first of them, the Herkomer Trophy, was indeed a coæval of the TT, being first staged in August 1905. It was organized by a well-known German-born portrait painter, Hubert von Herkomer, who had lived in England for many years and shared the concern for the development of the fast comfortable touring car rather than the racer. Held on a road circuit running from München to Baden-Baden and back, the Herkomer Trophy immediately became an important sporting and social event: one of the competitors in 1906, at the wheel of a 40-horsepower Benz similar to the winning car, was no less an enthusiast than Prince Heinrich of Prussia.

After the third and last Herkomer event was held in 1907, the Prince himself instituted a series of quite stiff sporting trials to be held annually in his name. The route was Alpine, the regulations strict, the performance required would have done credit to an outright racing car very few years earlier, and yet the vehicles had to wear practical and efficient touring bodies. In fact it was the standards set in this difficult event which really gave birth to the idea of the sports car as we eventually came to know it, a compact and lightly-built yet comfortable car that could be driven on ordinary roads and driven fast. Historians of the British motor industry like to regard the Prince Henry Vauxhall as their primordial sports car, even though by continental standards it was not especially lively: the Vauxhall proved capable of 72 mph, but the Benz could reach 80, and both were put firmly in the shade by the Austrian Daimlers (later to be called Austro-Daimlers) designed by Herr Ferdinand Porsche: these were superb cars with efficient overhead-camshaft 5·7-litre engines, beautifully balanced chassis, and clever-tulip-shaped bodies that minimized the frontal area while staying within the rules, and they were capable of nearly 90 mph. They utterly dominated the 1910 event, which thereafter lapsed, its place in the scheme of things being assumed by the Austrian Alpine Trial from which the modern Alpine Rally was to emerge in 1929. This was an event which undoubtedly showed off the sports car to best advantage, and there is no doubt that it served its purpose in developing early concepts of high-performance road cars: the Rolls-Royce Silver Ghost might never have had a 4-speed gearbox but for its ignominious failure to climb one of the hills in the Austrian Alpine Trial.

Climbing steep hills, darting around corners, and rushing pell-mell along country roads, came naturally to the new generation of sporting road cars whose evolution in mainland Europe during the years preceding the Great War seemed positively Darwinian. Things were rather different in Great Hippophile Britain, where it was held both immoral and illegal to exceed 20 mph on the public highway – what do they know of limits, who only limits know? – and 'motor racing' meant the track at Brooklands.

Three lines of evolution for the sports car. The Prinz Heinrich trials produced some notable 'Prince Henry' models from Austro-Daimler, Vauxhall and others. The Métallurgique of 1908 (top left) was among the less successful. Below it, a scene from the Isle of Man in 1914, when the TT was run over two days with 300 miles on each, and this Straker-Squire was defeated by Sunbeam. On this page, approaching the sports car more modestly if no less adventurously, one of the 23 starters in the original 1911 Monte Carlo Rally. The winning Turcat-Méry was one of the Paris starters; others came from Brussels, Berlin or Vienna.

Brooklands bred some brutish battlewagons: this S76 Fiat driven by Sig. Pietro Bordino was known as the 'Brooklands 300hp'.

Neighbours called it 'the horrid motor track' and were militant in protesting against the danger to the district's amenities that it threatened. They eventually enforced the use of silencers, and the prohibition of racing at night, and were generally antagonistic to motorists – though not so much to the pioneer aviators who used the aerodrome within the track. Motorists elsewhere were enthusiastic, and the motoring press was properly deferential. This account of the opening of the track was in the same issue of The Motor *as carried a report of Fiat's domination of the Kaiserpreis.*

This entirely artificial motor course was built with the sweat of a couple of thousand navvies and horses, and with a substantial portion of the private fortune of Mr. H. F. Locke King. His idea, for which he was prepared to give so much of his estate both literally and metaphorically, was to provide the British motor industry with a proving ground where cars, motorcycles, and other vehicles, could be tested unhindered by speed limits and the generally hostile police. Obviously the track could serve also as a racing venue, and it was almost certainly that prospect which encouraged the astonishingly rapid completion of the construction, which involved diverting a river in two places, demolishing farms, felling a lot of timber and moving a vast amount of earth. The design of the track was entrusted to Colonel Capel Holden of the Royal Engineers, who had earlier attracted some fame for his bridges and some interest in his motorcycles. He laid out the Brooklands track as a pair of constant-radius banked turns linked by a half-mile straight and another strip of flat concrete track with a reverse curve in it. Its width was 100 feet, its lap distance three and a quarter miles, and its hurried and somewhat shallow construction was to make it notoriously bumpy. At the same time, its super-elevated or banked corners made it possible for the cars of the time and some time afterwards to drive flat-out all the way around the circuit, which was fine for testing the mechanical stamina of a car but bore little or no relationship to motoring usages in the real world. Hitherto, motor racing had been road racing, sometimes all too realistic in its presentation of everyday hazards magnified by extraordinary speeds. Brooklands turned motor racing into a circus act. That was enough to bring the crowds; but the organizers could advertise that it attracted 'The right crowd, and no crowding'. Tucked away in a sequestered middle-class district that was then barely close enough to London to constitute a suburb, Brooklands liked to think that it was nearer to Ascot than to Epsom Downs. Undoubtedly the thinking was in those horsey terms for, in the early days of the track, horse-racing procedures were adopted so automatically that the concrete saucer might have been a turf tureen. The cars were not numbered, but their drivers wore jockey's silks in their entrant's colours; the driver was a hired hand, not a gentleman. The races were even started by Mr. Hugh Owen, formerly starter to the Jockey Club. All the races were short sprints, nearly all of them conducted on a handicap basis that allowed a nonsensically heterogeneous assortment of cars to compete with each other, and which negated all mechanical progress since the only way of doing better with the passage of time was to fool the handicappers – and the chief of these throughout almost the entire history of the track was Mr. A. V. Ebblewhite, who was nobody's fool.

Brooklands was a marvellous place in its way, especially after the organizers showed some horse sense and got rid of all the horse nonsense. The aviation, the atmosphere, the facilities, even the quality of the

Interesting features of England's first motor speedway :—

> **The track measures 2¾ miles.**
>
> **Its average width is 100 feet.**
>
> **At the fork where the kilometre straight for finishing leaves the main track, the measurement is 250 feet.**
>
> **The banking on the curves is 27 feet 6 inches.**
>
> **Speeds of 90 to 100 miles per hour are possible.**
>
> **The track is adjacent to Weybridge Station on the L. & S.W. main line.**

The Track Opened.

THE motor speedway, which has been under construction at Weybridge for some time, and concerning the progress of which readers of "THE MOTOR" have been informed from time to time, was inspected yesterday (Monday) by the Press and other visitors.

The special train contained a large number of Pressmen and well-known automobilists. The day being beautifully fine a large number motored to the track, and there were about two hundred present at the luncheon, which was presided over by Mr. F. Locke-King. There was only one speech, made by Mr. King. He remarked that the course was barely ready, and he apologised for the fact, but they wanted to get it open that day, so as to be in good form for the big event of July 6th. He said that he thought the track was worth building, as it would act as a safety valve to the speed proclivities of automobilism. He mentioned several names of people who had given their assistance: Lord Montagu, who was the first to give the track a start J. W. Orde, Mr. Hugh Owen, and Col. Holden. Mr. King said that the track never could have been constructed without Mr. Holden's help, and that he did everything in his power to assist him. After luncheon there was a procession round the track of about 50 cars, all well-known makes. The procession was led by Mrs. Locke-King. Those present yesterday were:—Earl of Lonsdale, Lord Montagu, the Earl of Essex, the Duke of Westminster, Lord Allington, Lord Carnarvon, Colonel Holden, Col. Lindsay Lloyd, the Hon. F. Lowther, Hon. C. S. Rolls, Professor Boys, Mr. Max Pemberton, the Hon. Mrs. Assheton-Harbord, and others. After the procession there were tests by a number of well-known cars.

This country can now boast of having the first and largest purely motorcar racing track in the world. There have, of course, been speed races on improvised tracks, such as in the States, where many of the old horse-racing courses have been

Taking the banking at the new Brooklands motor-racing track.

converted into automobile racing tracks. However, the element of danger is always present on a makeshift course such as a horse track, the surface is soft (in America, as a rule, it consists of tan), the curves are sharp and flat, and totally unfit for speed work on a car; indeed, it is practically impossible to take the corners at a more than average speed without overrunning the track. This has been demonstrated time and again by the appalling number of fatal accidents that have occurred on American car racing tracks, and is even exemplified in the report of a 24-hours' race in this issue. A mere glimpse at Brooklands speedway, however, shows at once that it has been scientifically constructed for the fastest speeds, at the same time ensuring the utmost safety of the steersman. The new motor-racing centre may be approached by several routes from London, but probably the most direct is via Cobham, and, taking the road to Chertsey straight ahead at the top of Pain's Hill, just beyond Cobham, instead of the main road bearing to the left, which leads to Ripley. About a mile and a half brings one to the main entrance of the track. An alternative route is by Kingston, along the Portsmouth Road as far as Winters Bridge, and turn sharp to the right, passing Imber Court, to Walton, leading to Weybridge. The former is the better way, in our opinion. Either the main entrance can be taken at Weybridge, or a short cut along Brooklands Lane. The latter road, however, is more to be recommended for pedestrians than cars, as the highway at present consists of the most vile "corduroy" road.

What the Track is Like.

It is barely nine months ago that work was commenced in earnest, and to-day the great motor racecourse stands completed —a colossal monument to the conceptive genius and courage of its founder. Bare figures convey no sense of its stupendous size, and words must fail to describe the impression that the finished track creates at first view. There was a sense of vastness about it during the preparatory work, but the long white ribbon that winds round the green land in the centre seems, in the distance, to merge into the horizon, appears far longer when denuded of the group of busy labourers. In its nakedness one finds no measure of its size. As it lies, the inner edge of the track, which is 100ft. wide, measures nearly 2¾ miles.

In shape the course is ovaloid, the two curves that join the straight runs at the side being laid out each to a different radius, in one case 1,500ft., in the other 1,000ft. Round the curves the track is banked up to a height of about 27ft. 6in., 18in. more than was provided in the designs, the extra amount having been added as an allowance for the settling of the earth. During the progress of the work rails were laid down for the transport of material, and it is thought now that the

NEWS.—Contd.

traffic which passed during that period will have sufficed to conglomerate the foundation. No fear of any settling is entertained, and the concrete facing is expected to remain in good condition. In this connection it is worthy of note that, whereas the designs showed a maximum gradient of 1 in 2 at the top of the bank, the actual maximum is 1 in 1.6. On the supposition that no friction exists between the rubber tyres of the wheels and the concrete, the banking, as designed, was steep enough to permit a speed of 90 miles per hour with perfect safety. Under the present conditions this figure has risen to 120 miles per hour. This provides a very large margin of safety, because there is friction between the wheels and the track to resist lateral motion. There are no reliable data upon which to base a calculation of the highest speed that will safely be attainable, but it may

be said that no car is likely to be built for many years to come which will not be able to negotiate the curves at full speed.

How the actual distances on the complete lap will be measured has not yet been decided. Obviously, a car of 20h.p. taking the curves near the inner edge will not cover such a long distance on each round as a racer of 120h.p., which will be obliged to run higher up the bank. This is one of the points that will be determined during the trial period before July 6th, when the first race meeting will be held. There may be a line 10ft. from the inner edge, and another in the centre of the track. The greatest error will probably never exceed 100ft. per mile, even if no allowance is made for cars of different speed. Diagonally across the oval course

A STRAIGHT RUN HAS BEEN LAID OUT FOR KILOMETRE RECORDS

and for finishing races. At the fork where this leaves the main track there is a width

of 250ft., and the angle of divergence is so small that a driver going round the course at a high speed can run with equal ease along either. Not only is this necessary to permit cars to get up their best pace before flying attempts at records are made, but also to enable competitors to finish in front of the stands, which are situated on a hill overlooking not only the straight but the greater portion of the course, only a short section of the curve which runs behind the hill being invisible. Between the judges' box on the straight and the spot where the main track is again rejoined there is a distance of 300 yards, with a gradient of 1 in 12, and should this not suffice for pulling up a car, there is an easy bend to the curve of the main track. Situated on the inner side of this dead level kilometre straight is the clubhouse and competitors' enclosure, which contains covered stalls to the number of 75 for competing machines. Besides the offices in the clubhouse, there is a large

GUY LIPSCOMBE

A general view of the Brooklands motor speedway at Weybridge, which was officially opened yesterday (M... has been able to keep out of the picture. Inset shows the angle of the banking. Centre track

NEWS.— *Contd.*

Press gallery, a stewards' observation tower and the weighing-room.

Already seating accommodation for 5,000 people has been provided, the stands, part of which are covered, extending in terraces down the slope of the hill. There is standing room also for 150,000 people in front of and below the stands. Separate enclosures, each with their own dining-rooms, are provided for members and for visitors paying different entrance fees. Pine trees overshadow the top of the hill, and the walks are covered with crushed shells. Access to the hill is obtained either by a bridge spanning the track or by a road leading through a tunnel under the track, the main object of which is to allow motoring spectators to drive their cars to a special enclosure on the hill out of sight of the stands. From the stands the names of the competitors in each race will be visible on a large board in the Club en-closure, which is right opposite the stands.

With regard to the racing rules, it may be said that the only special regulations made in addition to those of the R.A.C., compel cars to be driven round the course in a left-handed direction, to pass all cars or obstacles on the right, and permit competitors only to stop their cars in the refuges provided on the inside of the track. There are seven signal boxes or observation stations at different points, with a refuge near each, and all being in telephonic communication with the central clubhouse, the officials can be quickly apprised of any circumstances that may need their instant attention. Although the track is at present

WREATHED IN THE GLAMOUR OF THE COMING RACES,

the fact must not be overlooked that its chief use will be as a trial ground, not only for manufacturers who desire to test their models, but for their customers, who may wish to have ample demonstration of the capabilities of their cars. It is with this object in view that 28 garage houses have been erected close by the tunnel road leading to the Club enclosure. For a small rental any one of these may be reserved by a firm for its own use. On the vast green centre enclosed by the track it is the intention of the owners to construct test hills of different grades. When these will have been completed the Brooklands course will form an ideal testing venue, where it will be possible, without danger, to try a car to the fullest extent. Except on Sundays and those days for which race meetings have been announced, when the track will, of course, be reserved for the Brooklands Automobile Club, any motorist, on payment of a small fee, will be able to take his car on the course. Every morning of this week, for instance, the two Weigel racing machines, which cannot be properly tested at full speed on the road, will spend an hour on the track.

Our artist's drawing shows the track as no photograph can depict it, because of obstructions which the artist ...hing straight. On the right of straight is the clubhouse. On the left the judge's box will be seen.

The Motor *criticized American dirt tracks. Mr. Joe Dawson seems happy to have finished the race for the 1910 Savannah Challenge Trophy, winning with his Marmon on what purported to be roads.*

light, all seemed special. So they were, and many a racing man, mechanic, tuner, builder, engineer, driver, or mere hopeless case, might spend his lifetime striving within its pear-shaped perimeter. Since its bumps were practically the only things that inhibited sustained full-throttle running, lap times were basically a function of the relative vulnerabilities of the engine's bearings and the driver's kidneys. The rest of the automotive world shook its head sadly at this characteristically English display of what Jan Hus might have called 'Unholy Simplicity', and then got on with the business of learning how to make cars that would not only go, but would also steer and stop.

The Americans soon lost interest in all that. They had toyed with Grand Prix motor racing in the Savannah Grand Prize, run from 1908 according to European formulae, and had experimented on the lines of the Gordon Bennett Cup in the races for the Vanderbilt Cup which began in 1904. Their early popularity was not long maintained, possibly because the early winners were European. In any case the niceties of high-speed cornering were lost on a nation like America in the dawn of motoring, when either you drove on the predominantly straight main highways and you just went, or you drove off them and you went, but only just. What could tail slides or four-wheel drifts mean in a country where the domestic motor industry built all its cars with the same 4 ft 8½ inch track so that they could all run in the same ruts? America might need motor racing, but it did not appear to need road racing; what it needed was a closed-circuit track, and

This was supposed to be a road, when the 1914 Vanderbilt Cup was raced for at Santa Monica; and this upset was typical.

one Carl G. Fisher found financial backing for the construction of a suitable track on the outskirts of Indianapolis, Indiana. The course was rectangular, two and a half miles to the lap, made up of two long straights of 5/8ths of a mile, two shorter ones of 1/8th of a mile and four identical $\frac{1}{4}$ mile turns banked at a shade over nine degrees from the horizontal. In August 1909 it was ready; but within less than three days of racing the surface had broken up so badly that racing had to be abandoned. Four inches of gravel limestone and tar were simply not good enough. It took nearly three and a quarter million paving bricks, 155,000 dollars, and sixty-three days to correct that mistake, and then it was winter – but not too cold for Lewis Strang to average nearly 92 mph for two laps of the circuit in his Buick, which was unofficially clocked at nearly 112 mph along the straight.

When the weather brightened, so did Fisher's prospects. The crowds swarmed in and offered the racers and their cars even more uncritical adulation than the crowds at Brooklands. The honeymoon did not last long, for there were too many races for most of them to matter, and the promoters finally decided to concentrate their 1911 efforts on one big race to be held on Memorial Day, 30 May. Eventually they decided on a distance of 500 miles (so that it could be concluded during daylight) and thus was born the richest, brightest, most ballyhooed, and occasionally most frightening, motor race in history, a race almost as long in span as motor-racing history itself.

Mr. Berna Eli ('Barney') Oldfield ready for the start on a brick surface in a car equally typically American.

By 1915 American racing was done on formal arenas (car number 4 above is the 1914 Mercédès which won at Indianapolis and Elgin in 1915); real road racing was to be found in Sicily, still as natural as when this remarkably theatrical picture opposite was taken during the Targa Florio race of 1907.

One race a year in Indiana is not going to do much for 150 million Americans. Neither would three and a quarter million paving bricks do much for the finances of any entrepreneur seeking to emulate Fisher. What happened instead was that a series of circular or oval banked wooden tracks began to proliferate around the United States, the first being built in 1910 at Playa del Rey, near Los Angeles, the rest following in fairly rapid order from 1915 onwards. They seldom lasted long, having been built with all the economy that treads in the shadows of speculation: after three years or so they were usually in need of costly repair, in which case they were allowed to succumb to the rival pressures of the popular dirt tracks, or they were sold as real estate for building development in highly populated areas, or they mysteriously caught fire. Occasionally a kindly nature intervened to dispose of such embarrassments: a board track in Florida was destroyed by a hurricane. While they lasted, however, they gave the public thrills aplenty and speed galore, the lap times at some of them being substantially faster than those recorded at Indianapolis. The cars that reached these speeds were initially a very mixed bunch, European as well as domestic, but gradually they all became very similar as specialization set in, and finally the racing became as irrelevant to motoring as it had been at Brooklands. The main difference was that the board tracks were less bumpy.

Bumps? Even the Brooklands habitués did not know the worst of them. They should have tried the route of the Targo Florio in Sicily, a race which was inaugurated in 1906 and which somehow survived to the 1970s as the last of the great road races. It really was a road race – and such roads! Even by the standards

Longest-lived of the great road races, the Targa Florio
grew out of a devoted motorist's understanding of what was
really necessary for a car to be driven quickly. It encouraged
cars that were agile but not unstable, cars with the best
possible steering and braking and roadholding, with
adequate strength and ample stamina; it discouraged cars
that were grossly heavy or grotesquely underpowered. As
for the Sicilian onlookers, they encouraged an Italian win –
or, better still, a Sicilian one.

The 1907 Targa Florio was one of the three races that Fiat carried off in their magnificent hat-trick that year. Car 20 A is brought to the line by the team's fastest driver, already planning the construction of his own Lancia car. Below, at the end of the Coppa Florio (founded by the same person, but held at Brescia) in 1907, the winner Minoia and his mechanic discuss their dusty drive in an Isotta-Fraschini, a car similar to that shown on page 61.

of the early 1900s when all roads were pretty rough, those of Sicily were downright rotten; and by the standards of the Sicilians, there were parts of the Targa Florio circuit that were best left to mountain goats, preferably bullet-proof ones. Bandits were as great a hazard as bumps, and it was not unknown for competitors to carry sidearms, just in case. What a car from Brooklands or the board tracks would have made of the circuit, goodness only knows; but the Italian manufacturers, who were most attracted to the event, understood perfectly what was required. In that country motor sport had already become an almost religious passion; and one of the most devoted of its followers was Vincenzo Florio, the youngest son of a prosperous and well-known family of merchants in Sicily. He owned one of the first cars on the island, he befriended racing drivers, and he had a go at competition driving himself before the family made it plain that he was taking his irresponsibilities too seriously. Thereafter he became a patron of motor racing: the Coppa Florio was run on the mainland, up north near Brescia, as early as 1900, and then the magnificent Targa Florio was created. It was in these its earliest days that it was perhaps at its most daunting, being run on the longest of the three different circuits used in the history of the race. All three, Great, Medium and Short, bore the name of the Madonie mountains, into which the route climbed more than 3000 ft above sea level, twisting, turning, diving and swooping around fields and hillsides, through villages and towns, slamming down into some rustic market place and rocketing out again as though seeking better fare, finally dropping down to sea level for the long fast coastal straight, running three miles alongside the Tyrrhenian Sea, west of Campofelice. Three laps of this circuit amounted to 277 miles, and it took all the precision and delicacy of Alessandro Cagno to keep his monster Itala on the roads at an overall average speed of 29 mph, to win the 1906 race by more than half an hour. Most of the great drivers of this age were burly men, fit to wrestle with their giant mounts on a fairly even basis; Cagno was one of those rare and gifted drivers, slight of build and sensitive of touch, directing their cars with microscopic accuracy, by feel rather than by force. He drove Fiats for most of his racing career, but at this time he was being employed for two or three seasons by Itala, and that company profited greatly from his services.

Nevertheless it was a Fiat that won in the following year, driven by no less a man than the great Felice Nazzaro who, as it happened, had for some time been a personal driver to Vincenzo Florio. That was a great year for the Turin company, and indeed a great year for motor racing; and as we shall see, Nazzaro and the Fiat prospered equally in the most important race of the year, the Grand Prix of the ACF. This and the Sicilian race were for broadly the same kind of cars, big blasting battlewagons that we should nowadays suppose crude blunderers, though we should be wrong. The Targa Florio would continue in this vein, as a

Above, one of the winning Fiat team in the pits during the 1907 Grand Prix de l' ACF at Dieppe. Below, the almost uncontrollable front-wheel-drive Christie that took part in the same event. Its V4 engine of 19 litres was the largest ever to run in a Grand Prix; its American designer/driver Mr. J. Walter Christie ran a New York ironworks, and was a pioneer in the construction of military tanks.

remote and curiously rustic echo of the Grands Prix of its day (a pre-echo perhaps, since the first race in Sicily preceded the/first Grand Prix by a matter of fifty days) until in 1936 it became a sports car event, for reasons that will be appreciated when we reach that juncture in our history. The Grands Prix proper, however, immediately became the standard-setters, the criteria against which all other motor racing achievements might be measured. There was at first nothing special about the competitors to justify this assumption of superiority; it was really a political affair, a product of the rabid nationalism which infected France even more than most other supposedly civilized countries.

The plain fact was that the French were fed up with the restrictions of the Gordon Bennett races. As had been obvious in the elimination trials that they had been forced to conduct in 1904 and 1905, the French were in a position to field more competent racing cars than practically all the other competing nations put together, and they failed to see why they should not do so. To be limited to three cars, no more than the quota allowed from Germany, Britain, Belgium or even Switzerland, seemed to the Automobile Club de France an insult to the fertility of the nation's brains. What was more, the freedom to field a large entry brought with it the increased probability of a French victory; and according to the dictates of the national spirit, victory by a French car was far more important to Gallic self-respect than any considerations of sportsmanship, fair play, or technical merit – in all of which the French blandly assumed themselves supreme anyway. They had won the 1905 Gordon Bennett race, and were therefore to stage the 1906 one, but they could not be compelled to honour such an obligation. The donor of the Cup might well be living in Paris, and indeed spending there a good deal of his stupefying stipend; but he was nevertheless more than welcome to offer his name and benefactions to some other sport. He did: the next Gordon Bennett Trophy was for ballooning – and the next international motor race of comparable importance was the new Grand Prix d l'ACF.

It was held at Le Mans on a 64-mile circuit that, in plan if not in scale, was the model for many future motor races based on provincial towns. Roughly triangular, it departed along one of the tolerably straight and mildly undulating major roads radiating from the town, eventually turning into a shorter leg composed of much more sinuous and less well-surfaced minor roads which eventually led to another main road returning by a convergent route to the town. The surfaces varied, here dusty, there stony, and in one stretch wooden planks served as a hastily-built bypass to avoid the innocent little village of St. Calais. This mixture had to be negotiated six times on each of two consecutive days. Thirty-two cars started, at 90-second intervals, and they represented three countries and thirteen makes, of which no less than ten were French.

The German teams were highly drilled for the 1908 Grand Prix. Pitwork by Benz, above, was typical. In 1907, fuel consumption was strictly measured under the supervision of the Chevalier de Knyff, here checking the Lorraine-Dietrich of M. Fernand Gabriel.

All of the cars were big, being generally similar to the cars participating in the 1905 Gordon Bennett race, with the surprising exception of the Renault, which was of a simpler and more conventional design than the technically very advanced 1905 car. What made their size all the more remarkable was that it was achieved in spite of regulations which limited the weight of a racing car to a tonne, a rule that had been introduced in 1902 in an attempt to prevent racing cars from becoming too fast. It was the first but certainly not the most ineffectual of many times when an attempt to limit the performance of racing cars by introducing some strictly irrelevant constraint was shown to be mere folly, and to amount to nothing more than a challenge to the engineering ability of racing car constructors. Consider for example that the racing Panhard of 1901, which weighed 1·2 tonnes, had an engine of $7\frac{1}{2}$ litres, whereas its successor in the following year had a 13·7-litre engine in a car weighing one tonne. This was truly the age of Titans, a period in which long and arduous races were fought out on rudimentary roads by cars of gigantic proportions, abysmal efficiency, little scope for development, but surprisingly good balance. Another surprise was their quite comfortable ride, a privilege that later racing drivers were to be denied for half a century, and due to the general use of chain-drive to the rear wheels and to the absence of brakes on the front wheels, so that unsprung weight was relatively slight and fairly soft springs could be employed. Yet although the ride of these cars were good, drivers were severely fatigued by the heaviness of the controls, so heavy sometimes that drivers had been known to fail to negotiate a corner due to their sheer inability to force the steering round as much as was

GRAND PRIX DE L'A. C. F.
CIRCUIT DE LA SEINE-INFÉRIEURE
hevalier de Kniff mesurant l'essence de la Lorraine-Diétrich 2

necessary. Making things worse for them was the sheer length of the races (the driver of the winning car in the 1906 Grand Prix was at the wheel for 12 hours 14 minutes, spread over two days) and the gruelling work involved in changing tyres – an undertaking that had to be faced with intimidating frequency, for the tyres of these cars were quite unable to sustain the loads, speeds, and abrasion, to which they were subjected, for anything like long enough to see through a day's racing.

These tyres were made of natural rubber of dubious and inconsistent quality, reinforced with zinc oxide which gave them their characteristic whiteness, superimposed on a cotton carcass, and anchored by beads in the edges of the wheel rim. When a tyre failed it had to be removed by main force or, more quickly, by being slashed away with the big and frighteningly sharp knife which was part of the riding mechanic's tool kit; the old tyre had then to be replaced with a fresh one at some considerable cost in muscular effort and in mangled fingers. The situation was aggravated by the regulations for the 1906 Grand Prix, which insisted that tyres could only be changed by the men travelling in the car, without assistance from others. This was countered by the introduction of detachable wheel rims, which proved their worth when the winning driver changed all four tyes in 3 minutes 47 seconds half way through the first day.

That driver was the Hungarian Ferenc Szisz at the wheel of the new if retrograde Renault. This car, like all the others in the race that mattered, had a four-cylinder engine of more than 12 litres displacement (the Panhard had a capacity of no less than 18 litres) and when timed through a kilometre on the grandstand straight it was found to be the fastest of all at a speed of 92·4 mph. Notwithstanding this, the driving of Szisz was a model of restraint; and notwithstanding that, his average speed of 63 mph for the two days gave him victory by a clear margin over the Fiat which was his nearest rival. The differences between the two cars illustrated the differences in national characteristics; the French had the best, longest, straightest major roads, their proudly Napoleonic *Routes Nationales*; the Italians, while enjoying the level straights of the flat Po plain at the front door of their Torino factory, were conscious of the Alps at the back door, and so although the Fiat might be deficient in outright speed compared with the Renault, its superiority in acceleration and stability would stand it in good stead in any race run on a more sinuous course, as 1907 was to demonstrate.

Giants though they were, the cars of this period were often so finely proportioned as to belie their stature; and few examples better illustrate this harmonious balance than the 16·2-litre Fiat which won the Grand Prix de l'ACF in 1907. Nor was this balance illusory or merely visual: many of these cars were endowed with such stability, cornering power, and nicety of steering as could not be equalled by the

The Dieppe circuit used for the races of 1907 and 1908 was employed again in 1912, when the 7.6-litre Peugeot revolutionized racing car design. The Sunbeam seen opposite was a 3-litre car entered in the simultaneous Coupe de L'Auto race for light cars. The course used for the 1914 race near Lyon was over more adventurous roads, the view on pages 74–5 showing the winding descent to Les Sept Chemins, at the end of a long straight where the fastest cars exceeded 105 mph.

majority of Grand Prix cars in the next two decades.

The merits of the Fiat – which should not by their perspective appear to diminish those of that company's leading driver, Signor Felice Nazzaro – were amply demonstrated in 1907, for it was by contemporary motor-racing standards a rather busy one. The French organizers of the 1906 Grand Prix hastened to promote it afresh in 1907, while the Germans created an event of their own, intended to attract ordinary cars rather than specialized racers and doubtless conceived with a view to putting the French in their places. Furthermore the Italians proposed again to run their race in Sicily for the Targa Florio, as in the previous year, a race which imposed the severest demands on the roadworthiness of the cars and one in which the victor was correspondingly held in high esteem.

All three of these races were of major importance; all three were very well supported, perhaps better than ever before; and all three were won in a convincing display of superiority by Fiat. What made this performance remarkable is that the three races were governed by different formulae, and the Torinese firm fielded entirely different cars for each event. In the case of the German race for the *Kaiserpreis*, the biggest engine allowed was 8 litres and the minimum weight 1175 kg; in Sicily the rules were based, like so many fiscal systems of the time, on piston area; and in France there was only the stipulation that fuel consumption would be limited to 30 litres for 100 kilometres. It was for this last that Fiat contrived a large but very lightly stressed 16·2-litre engine, the car averaging better than 9·4 miles per gallon while defeating thirty-seven starters to win the French Grand Prix in six and three quarter hours at an average speed of 70·5 mph.

That race was significant in a couple of other respects. For the first time, the competing cars were required to be painted in the racing colours allotted to their respective nations – green for England (a matter which gave the superstitious much cause for complaint and many excuses for failure), red for Italy, white for Germany, blue for France, yellow for Belgium, red and yellow for Switzerland, red and white for the United States of America. If this had the deplorable effect of maintaining and indeed heightening the spirit of nationalism that was all too swiftly overtaking the sport of motor racing, at least it had also the virtue of making the 1907 GP Renault distinguishable from the otherwise identical 1906 version, which had been painted red. In 1907 it was the Renault faces that were red, for Szisz finished with over six and a half gallons of fuel unused; had he driven less circumspectly and allowed his motor to consume its fuel more avidly, he might have made up the seven minutes deficit whereby he finished second.

The other interesting sidelight on the race is that the Mercédès team was as early as this being subjected to a strict control. The crews attended lectures in which they were instructed not only in the niceties of their

machines and the exigencies of the circuit but also on the features whereby they might recognize their rivals on the road (not an easy thing to do when peering through the dust clouds left by a preceding car) and even the weaknesses and foibles of rival drivers, with hints on how these might be exploited. The Germans were even more efficient in 1908 when the race was again held, as in 1907, at Dieppe, and Mercédès even used pneumatic jacks for wheel changes at the pits. They were a good investment, for the roads were in poor condition and all the competitors suffered grievous delays while dealing with punctured tyres. The winner, a former locksmith's apprentice named Christian Lautenschlager (drivers representing Germany no longer had to be high-born, though no doubt it helped), drove with some caution to achieve his first major victory, and yet had to stop nine times for tyre replacements. Others stopped as many as nineteen times. The popular detachable rims on wooden spoked wheels made a tyre-change quicker and less painful than in the years before 1907; but when Napier proposed to race their Grand Prix cars with detachable wire wheels, whose removal and replacement would be much faster even than was possible with those detachable rims, they were condemned as unsound by the ACF who showed (not for the first time, nor the last) that they could readily allow political and patriotic issues to obscure their technical judgement.

It would be unfair, however, to blame the ACF for the fact that, after France's entries had taken such a beating in 1907 and 1908, they did not hold their Grand Prix in 1909. What actually happened was that the principal French and German manufacturers conspired to boycott all long-distance races, which they found increasingly burdensome. It was undoubtedly the Club that was to blame in 1910, or more particularly the senior French manufacturers who dominated the Club and who would not foster a race which might, as seemed quite likely, be won by one of the many younger and technically more adventurous companies who had blossomed out in France. These young firms who, like the French public, were avid for more and freer racing, pursued instead the honours that could be won in the voiturette class, and in particular in the series of races for the Cup presented annually by the newspaper *L'Auto*. Here for the next few years was where the seeds of future technical evolution and revolution were germinated.

When the ACF revived their Grand Prix for 1912 they allowed a concurrent race for cars of less than 3 litres displacement and weighing more than 800 kilogrammes, which would compete for a *Coupe de l'Auto*; and no less than forty-two of the fifty-six runners were engaged in this substructural struggle. Of the remaining fourteen, the majority had very large engines, of perhaps 14 or 15 litres; but the new GP Peugeot mustered only 7·6 litres, being based on a design for a 1911 race that never took place. That design was, at least *prima facie*, the work of a young Swiss engineer called Ernest Henry, whose engine combined a number

of already proven ideas in an entirely original manner. These included twin overhead camshafts operating four valves inclined to match cross-flow porting of approximately hemispherical combustion chambers, and this new concept ought to have made the engine extraordinarily efficient by the standards of the time. Alas, the bottom half of Henry's very tall and very slim engine was altogether less clever, and so the Peugeot did not reach such high engine revolutions as its valvegear ought to have made possible. Hence it developed no more power than the big bangers against which it raced – and indeed it was outstripped in the race by the Fiat, which itself was not significantly faster than the cars of earlier years. It was only due to the random incidence of misfortune in both the Fiat and Peugeot teams that one of the latter eventually won at a not very convincing speed. As luck would have it, it was the fastest car of the Peugeot team that was the only example to survive until the end of the second day's racing, whereas the only Fiat to survive was certainly not the fastest member of that team, and it finished second. Had it been the fastest Peugeot's petrol pipe that had broken, or if the fastest Fiat's had not, the old-fashioned car would have emerged victorious in the Grand Prix, the expectations of Peugeot and Henry might have been confounded, and the lessons inferred from the event for application to car design in the future might have been entirely different.

Progress in engineering may appear systematic, but its direction is too often fortuitous. What it amounted to in this case was that a new kind of racing car became fashionable, substantially lighter and smaller than its predecessors, and having to work much harder in order to do no better than they did. Very soon, however, as the skills of bearing manufacturers and metallurgists were more effectively recruited to the cause, this new generation of cars began to do significantly better than the earlier race of giants, and the regulations governing Grand Prix racing were rapidly rejigged to give expression to the new thinking: by 1914 engine displacement was limited to $4\frac{1}{2}$ litres and the weight of the car had to fall between limits of 800 and 1100 kilogrammes.

That 1914 race remains memorable as one of the most passionately fought battles that nationalism ever imposed upon sport. It might have been seen as a contest between the Mercédès, which was undoubtedly faster, and the Peugeot which had the advantage of four-wheel brakes; it might have been seen as a contest between the stolid Christian Lautenschlager and the spirited Georges Boillot: but what it really amounted to was a straight fight between Germany and France, and in the end the German victory on French soil was received in icy silence, broken only by the ominous strains of *Deutschland uber Alles*. Soon the two nations were fighting a real war: Boillot sought his revenge in the air above the western front, and in 1916 he met his end there.

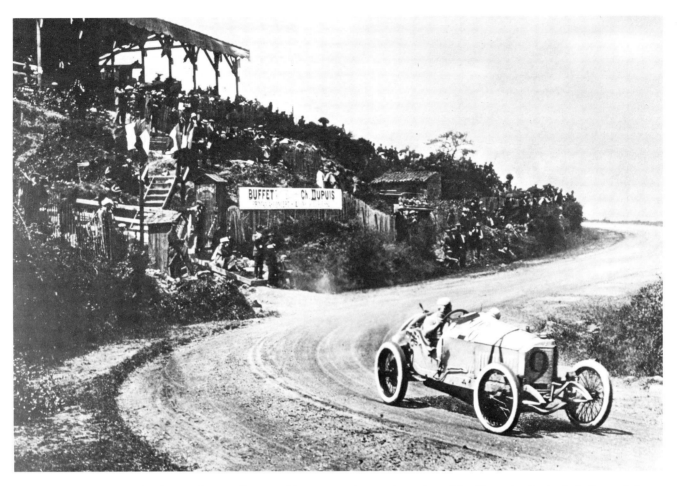

The end of an era: Mercédès driver Christian Lautenschlager swings his car down through les Esses *in the shocked silence of the crowd who were expecting their darling Georges Boillot to come first to the finish. Mercédès had beaten Peugeot; Germany had beaten France; and Germany would soon be at war with France . . .*

In 1915 the battle between the cars had been renewed, on the neutral territory of Indianapolis. The Italian-born American driver Ralph DePalma had managed to procure one of the Mercédès and get it on board ship before the outbreak of war, and he drove it in the 500-mile race at Indianapolis in May 1915. The only car to offer him serious resistance was a Peugeot driven by another expatriate Italian, Dario Resta (most of whose life was spent in England, where he was naturalized), but the Mercédès won by a clear five miles.

These and other European cars played a significant part in American racing during the years of the Great War, even to the extent that the proprietor of Indianapolis, Mr. Fisher, persuaded the Premier company to build three cars that were copies of the Peugeot. The straight-eight Ballot, another Henry design based on the principles he had expounded for Peugeot, figured prominently in the 1919 race, though as unluckily as Ballot's cars seemed always to do, and it was 1920 before American cars began to make the running. The winner then was a new 3-litre Frontenac entered as a Monroe-Frontenac and driven by Gaston Chevrolet who was born in France, the younger brother of the celebrated Louis Chevrolet who came from Switzerland. It was a Frontenac that won again in 1921, but this time it was driven by the one-eyed Thomas W. Milton and he was *really* American. Evidently a new age was dawning west of the Atlantic; but the same thing was happening on the east side.

CHAPTER TWO

CHAPTER TWO

TIME WILL RUN BACK AND FETCH THE AGE OF GOLD

1921–1934

These were the vintage years. There have been other periods when motor racing might have appeared to enjoy a golden age, others again when it might have best been described as copper-bottomed, gilt-plated, or guilt-ridden; but the 1920s and much of the 1930s saw a coalescence of technical and contextual traditions. A quite small number of engineering innovations, even fewer of which might be described as revolutionary, sufficed to see the racing car on its way for a generation and its engines in particular for seemingly ever. These vintage years were the time when Grand Prix cars were classically formulated, when the racing formula was often surprisingly free, and when the races themselves assumed a form that would still be recognizable today. These were the years, too, when the great sports-car races blossomed: some, like the Tourist Trophy, simply matured, while others (including notably the Mille Miglia and Le Mans) assumed majority virtually at birth. In America, whatever the quality of the racing, these were the years of America's noblest racing cars. And on both sides of the Atlantic, on sand and salt, men dismissed the familiar constraints of racing against each other and raced against time for the honour of being the fastest on earth.

It may be stretching the imagination a bit to draw a parallel between the first quarter of a century of motor sport and the first six days of creation. Nevertheless, had the Great Architect of motoring competition paused for a spot of stock-taking round about 1920, he might well have been contented with his labours and pronounced his work very good. Evolution and free will might yet play their parts, but it was all there. The light so lately reddened in the bloodshot eyes of war now fell golden again upon such men as were prepared to sublimate their competitive instincts in more creative ways. That light without which nothing wholesome grows fell with equal favour on road racing, track racing, record-breaking, and hillclimbing, all of them destined to spring up fast, grow strong, and prosper fast-rooted in the fruitful soil. It fell with equal

Pre-war cars loomed large in early post-war racing. Third in the 1921 Targa Florio was Cav. Giuseppe Campari in this Alfa Romeo 40/60 (below), basically a 1913 design. The winner (above) was Count Giulio Masetti in a 1914 GP Fiat; in 1922 he was to win again in a 1914 GP Mercèdes.

The most outstanding new post-war racing car was the 1921 GP Fiat. At its wheel sits Pietro Bordino, rated in his time 'the finest road-race driver in the world'.

benison on other forms of the sport whose seed would in time bear no less amazing fruit: on the long-distance reliability trials from which modern rallying fitfully grew, on the brief but explosive sprints along seaside promenades or through private parklands, in which modern drag racing might trace its forebears, and on the pulverized mess scattered sky-high from the dirt tracks where numberless nameless Americans sought and sometimes found a local notoriety while fathering what became modern stock-car racing in the NASCAR idiom; all these too burgeoned in the light of a new mechanical age, their roots deep in the earth's oil. The sun's amiable light was focused in the concrete saucer of Brooklands, just as it shimmered off the brickyard at Indianapolis. In Milano it warmed the terracotta of the Bicocca degli Arcimboldi, as it had done since about 1488 – and it added an altogether superfluous and probably unwelcome warmth to the adjacent mill rooms and vulcanizing shops, as it had done since 1897 when Pirelli started making bicycle tyres there, before embarking on car tyres to such good purpose that by the end of the 1913 motor racing season they could claim to have shod the winners of the French Grand Prix, the Coupe de l'Auto, the Giro di Sicilia (a clockwise 652-mile version of the Targa Florio), the Mont Ventoux hillclimb, and sundry other events of no mean significance. Thus emboldened they were now ready to take competition so seriously that in their future they were to enjoy two very long periods of supremacy in racing and another in rallying; and with the first of those periods initiated with wins in the 1919 and 1920 Targa Florio races, that future had already begun.

To the superficial observer, then, the future looked promising in the light of peace that had dawned on Armistice Day, 11 November 1918, and yet beneath this unruffled surface troubled currents were running. In fact the surface was a dashed sight too peaceful – those two races for the Targa Florio in 1919 and 1920 were the only races of any consequence to be run in Europe in those years, for England's Royal Automobile Club and the French manufacturers' association had got together shortly after the armistice and decided that, since neither of them wanted to be bothered with racing, there jolly well would not be any racing. Neither was there; no Tourist Trophy, no French Grand Prix, not even a Grand Prix of France – and there was a difference, the latter event being one that had been staged by a rival organization in 1912 and 1913. With France and Britain disengaged, that was virtually that, for Germany was simply ostracized by everybody except the Italians, and none of the other European nations had the spirit or motivation for

The ever stiffening rules of formal racing cramped the style
of engineers, but speed hillclimbs were very much free-style,
especially on the short sharp hills of England. Above, Carl
Jörns (driving for Opel, as he had since 1907) takes a class
win in the Bad-Kissingen hillclimb in 1922. Below,
Captain Archie Frazer-Nash (the N of GN, and later
the proprietor of Frazer Nash cars) flings the GN sprint
special known as 'Kim' into a corner at South Harting in 1921.

international competition, although they were content to have fun in little local events on their own ground. Anybody who was interested in racing – and certain French manufacturers certainly were – was looking westward towards America, where competition had continued year by year, where the racing was fast and the rewards rich.

A great change had come over motor racing. Its spirit was as different as that of the whole world after a war that had turned society upside down and given it a thorough shaking. The original Grand Prix races had been practically undisguised devices for maintaining French supremacy, as blatantly nationalistic as the Gordon Bennett affairs; but now the overriding motives were advertising and technical development. The latter might not have been a bad thing had it been decently husbanded, but it seemed that the whole world of motoring had got firmly into its silly head that big engines were necessarily more powerful than small ones and that, by imposing a capacity limit on the engines of racing cars, realism and morality and fair competition could all be maintained. All it meant was that engineers everywhere concentrated their efforts on creating highly-stressed fast-running engines of unprecedented complexity, with as many cylinders as they felt they could reliably put together. This was a trend that might have been forecast in 1914, when for the first time a capacity limit (4·5 litres) was imposed on Grand Prix cars; and by the time of the Indianapolis 500 miles race of 1919, the inevitable trend was beginning. A V12 Packard had been fastest of the lot so long as it stayed in one piece, and an old pre-war Peugeot had been fastest at the end after the deciduous teeth of all the opposition had been drawn, but the cars that made most of the running and attracted all the attention were 8-cylinder affairs, built in 101 days by Ballot. In 1920 it was much the same story, except that the capacity limit was now the international 3-litre one rather than the 300 cubic inch rule that the Americans had confected for themselves earlier. Ballot were there again with three straight-eights, and Duesenberg fielded four engines of the same sort. Before long you would not be able to pick your way through the racing workshops of any reputable manufacturer without barking your shins on a straight-eight engine waiting to be dropped into some poor chassis that needed at least as much reappraisal as the engine was getting.

There had in fact been a straight-eight or two in the Grand Prix of 1907. The chap who was really architect of the movement, however, was that extraordinary expatriate Italian artist cum engineer (one of the instinctive sort who had the good sense to pay qualified men well enough to do all his sums and to keep quiet about it) who had built a straight-eight back in 1911 by the simple expedient of sticking two of his little Type 13 four-cylinder engines together end to end. Seeing that one of those little 1·3-litre four-cylinder

On the previous page, Ralph DePalma in a Ballot at Indianapolis in 1921. The Ballot at the top of this page is the 2-litre model driven by Jules Goux in the 1922 Targa Florio. Below it, the complex 3-litre TT Vauxhall of 1922, at first a flop but later to do very well in private hands.

First American victory in a major European race went to this 1921 Duesenberg straight-eight. The engine was replaced by a Miller for the same car to win at Indianapolis in 1922.

engines in a correspondingly tiny car had run rings round all but one of the giants in the Grand Prix in France in 1911, this might have seemed a work of supererogation; but Bugatti was sufficiently taken with the idea to make straight-eight aero-engines during the Great War, and it was the influence they had on the brothers Duesenberg and on Ernest Henry that was responsible for the sudden eruption of straight-eight engines in motor racing after the war. Before long it would be Bugatti who seemed to bestride the racing world like some colossus – a feat which he encompassed without any undue stretching of the legs, for as well as producing cars of considerable merit and unquestionable beauty he also sold so many to private entrants that a few virtuoso voices raised by rival factory teams might well be drowned by the chorus.

Proponents of the 4-cylinder engine must have felt doomed at 'The Brickyard' in 1920, surrounded by a Chinese army of straight-eights, five of which were destined to finish in the first six. The Old Guard at Waterloo must have felt the same – but at Indianapolis it was the old guard that triumphed, America's winning Monroe being a Chinese copy of a 1913 Peugeot. Peugeot themselves had no further battle honours to add to their colours: the new 4-cylinder cars they built for the race, extraordinary affairs with five valves per cylinder and three camshafts, all failed. No Peugeot was ever to feature in a major race again.

Would the new world have to be summoned to redress the balance of the old? That was the old Monroe doctrine, but it was not the new Monroe that undertook the task; it was the Duesenbergs which came to France for the first Grand Prix to be run since 1914. The only opposition they were up against was that of the Ballot; and the race, like Waterloo, promised to be a damned close-run thing. The Duesenbergs, being American, only had 3-speed gearboxes; on the other hand they were introducing hydraulic brakes to racing, while Ballot's leading driver Ralph DePalma was still suspicious of ordinary four-wheel brakes and had the front ones of his car disconnected. In a race of attrition which proved nothing, a Duesenberg won

*Streamliners at Strasbourg: for the 1922 Grand Prix,
Ballot and Bugatti built bomb-shaped bodies, the former
(nearer the camera) being big enough in diameter to house a
spare wheel and tyre in the nose-piece ahead of the radiator.
Neither car was anywhere near fast enough to match the
winning Fiat.*

and a Ballot came second; either way it was a good day for straight-eights.

A better day was coming, and with it a better car. Later in 1921 there was another Grand Prix, a new Italian event staged at Brescia, and to it came a brand new Fiat that should have been at Le Mans for the preceding race. Even with another couple of months work behind it, it was not yet trouble-free; but while it ran it made the rest of the opposition look pitifully slow. Its engine was a straight-eight, but not like all the others: it had two valves per cylinder instead of four, and on its one-piece crankshaft were ten roller main bearings and eight similar big-ends, the sort of engineering that you do not attempt unless your racing shop occupies a couple of dozen fitters, every one of whom will swear that he is one of the only three men in all Italy who knows how to use a file properly. It was a prodigious engine, running even faster than the Duesenberg and developing even more power; and if it was a daring exercise it was also a costly one, for in the following year Grands Prix were to be for cars of not more than 2 litres displacement.

The 3-litre Fiat was not the car to beat, it was the car to copy.

Nobody was able to in the time available before the cars had to line up at Strasbourg for the 1922 French GP. Admittedly Bugatti's new car was a straight-eight, but there all resemblance ended: its bomb-shaped pseudo-streamlined body was like nothing on earth, unless it were the body of the competing 4-cylinder Ballot. As for Fiat, they turned up with a 6-cylinder engine which, like the rest of the car, was virtually a scaled-down and conveniently cropped version of the 1921 3-litre. Of course it was not terribly fast; none of the Grand Prix cars of that year was, for with their puny little 2-litre engines they were scarcely a match in acceleration and top speed for the 8-litre cars of 1908 – but the Fiat was so much faster than the others that, after it had averaged 79·2 mph for 6 hours 17 minutes to win, officials had to wait nearly an hour for completion of the same distance by the first of three Bugattis which were the only other cars to finish.

To say that the other competitors were discouraged by this performance would be like describing James Gordon Bennett as a man of comfortable means. Seldom if ever can the superiority of one car have been so overwhelming that three-quarters of its rivals preferred taunts of cowardice to proof of ineptitude. Yet this is what happened at the next race on the calendar, the 1922 Italian GP at Monza. Ballot, Bianchi, Delage, Rolland-Pilain, Sunbeam-Talbot-Darracq and, it is said, Benz and Mercédès, all forfeited their entry fees in the conviction that the Fiats would enjoy a runaway victory. Diatto was persuaded that valour was more honourable than discretion – an attitude that always characterized their designers who later became famous as the brothers Maserati – but their cars retired at quarter distance, leaving a sole Bugatti trailing to the finish hopelessly behind the team of Fiats.

Above left: at Monza for the 1922 GP meeting, Austro-Daimler fielded the Porsche-designed 1½-litre Sascha.
Below left: Giaccone ran fifth in the 1922 Targa Florio in a 1½-litre Fiat derived from the GP 2-litre.
Above: remember Count Masetti, pictured on page 82? Here he is in the 1914 GP Mercédès, winning the 1922 Targa Florio.
Mercédès were not wholly pleased; they had entered a team of new 2-litre cars, and had meant to win.

The 1923 Grands Prix: above left, the supercharged Fiat stops at the pits at Monza, and (below) hurtles past them at Tours. A lot less fast, and less powerful, the Voisin (above) was developed from a touring car to pioneer cuneiform streamlining at Tours.

That was when the head-hunting started. The success of the Fiat was fairly easily explained: the firm had at that time a technical office staffed by the most gifted team of design engineers that has ever been assembled. One should not believe everything one reads in the press, but in a newspaper interview Mr. Thomas Alva Edison, who might be presumed to know about such things, declared *Genius is one percent inspiration and ninety-nine percent perspiration*, in which case the drawing boards over which Guido Fornaca presided in principle and Carlo Cavalli in practice must have been the most sweat-stained in the industry. Under Cavalli, who came from a long line of distinguished lawyers, worked a superb team, all of whose names became legends: Bazzi, Becchia, Bertarione, Cappa, Jano, Massimino, and Zerbi. In a few years all but Cavalli and Zerbi would have deserted Fiat, having been wooed by other manufacturers who knew that an ounce of authenticity was worth a ton of mimicry. Thus the Fiat gospel was spread throughout the manufactories of Europe; but some of the head-hunters were in too much of a hurry, so some of the disciples were captured before Fiat had finished preaching. This happened to Sunbeam first and then to Alfa Romeo, but the latter recovered quickly and was not slow to emulate the next and greatest of the examples that Fiat set.

This was once again a straight-eight, still a 2-litre car as the regulations insisted and yet more powerful than the 3-litre of 1921. The important thing about it was that its engine was supercharged – and although it was not the first, it was the first to matter. Chadwick in America had done impressive things with the supercharger as early as 1908; Mercédès were trying unsuccessfully to do likewise in the Targa Florio of 1921; but the blown straight-eight Fiat, once it was working properly, was just as stupefying as the unblown Fiat 6 of the previous year, and thereafter every racing car of note in the next ten years would be fashioned in its image.

Weighing about 1550 pounds and capable of about 130 mph, the blown straight-eight Fiat was the fastest road racing car that the world had yet seen; but the world was not to see much of it, for Fiat virtually withdrew from racing in 1924. Almost simultaneously an almost identical car was fielded by Alfa Romeo, the beautiful model P2 designed by the former Fiat engineer Vittorio Jano. For the next few years this car was almost invincible, and certainly the most successful overall in Grand Prix racing. The only car seriously to rival it, the yet more beautiful and very much more original Type 35 Bugatti, generally proved its superiority only on particularly tight and demanding circuits where the Bugatti's superior roadholding, handling, braking,

The last time the Land Speed Record was set on an ordinary public road was in 1924. One of Fiat's biggest old bangers (its origins lay in 1908) was lengthened, christened Mephistopheles, *and driven by Brooklands habitué Ernest Eldridge III at 146.01 mph on a road at Arpajon in France.*

and steering, might do more than merely make up for the car's deficit in sheer power and straight-line speed. As might be expected, this difference showed up most vividly in the Targa Florio, which for some years became virtually a Bugatti preserve. The first two of Bugatti's run of five successes there were scored by just the right kind of driver: *He knew with unfailing accuracy at exactly what speed and in what manner each and every turn could be negotiated; the more difficult the road conditions, the more he drew away from his rivals by reason of his absolute and mathematical precision.* Thus wrote W. F. Bradley of Meo Costantini, one of Bugatti's official team drivers since 1924. This Italian belonged to a distinguished Venetian family and looked it: appreciably taller than his colleagues, noble of brow and finely chiselled of feature, he looked and was as patrician as the cars he drove – and when failing health prompted his retirement from the wheel he became Bugatti's racing manager in 1926 and stayed until 1935.

Those were years in which Grand Prix racing had a very chequered career. The governing formulae seemed to be changed every year or two, until by 1928 the manufacturers were so fed up that they and the majority of race organizers turned a completely blind eye to the regulations and ran under a sort of free-for-all formula that was not effectively superseded until 1934. About the only thing on which everybody was in agreement was that a Grand Prix was an important race and had to be over a significant distance. In the stiffly sprung cars of the time, running on surfaces that often left a lot to be desired, being ordinary public roads that had been closed for the occasion, the drivers might have been forgiven for feeling that an hour or two would be more than sufficient; but the least stern of contemporary critics would have dismissed that as a trivial sprint, barely long enough to get the car really hot, let alone to melt it. Any self-respecting race had to last for at least 300 miles, and more often than not it went on for longer, lasting for anything from five to as much as ten hours. It was hot work and hard: many a driver finished his stint with his hands blistered raw and bleeding from the fierce kick of the steering wheel as the imperfect steering geometry of the day reacted to the bumps on the road. His own organs might have reacted equally violently were they not corseted and restrained by a tight bodybelt, an item that several drivers thought scarcely less essential than gloves and goggles. Add to this discomfort the heat pouring into the cockpit from the engine compartment, the wind tearing and tugging at the head, arms, and clothing, the dust rising from the road as the surface broke up with the constant passage of the cars, and the shower of stones likely to be flung up by the rear wheels of any car that was being followed closely, and the racing driver's lot would appear a considerably less attractive and glamorous one than it was frequently made out to be. Great was the fame that attended the successful, however, for although Grand Prix racing might occasionally slip into the doldrums from year to year in this

period, motor racing overall enjoyed a tremendous boom in popularity, and in mainland Europe became one of the most popular sports. The great drivers' names were household, the arguments about their relative merits were commonplace, and the huge crowds attending the ever-increasing number of race meetings attested to a passionate enthusiasm which demonstrated that Europe was the true spiritual home of motoring.

This was certainly not due to motoring having become the normal means of locomotion for the ordinary man in the street. That still seemed an Utopian dream to the majority, and since the times were anything but stable in economic terms it might seem astonishing that so many should dream so much of something so seemingly unattainable. Paradoxical though it may seem, what may have attracted him to motor racing was its sheer realism. It was a wonderful time for the racing car, midway between the hyperthyroid gigantism of the early days, when a man might scarce aspire to climb up to the wheel, let alone to drive such a monster, and the latter days of overspecialized development that left the racing car knee-high to a corgi and too irrelevant for words. Protagoras had the right idea: *Man is the measure of all things*. The racing cars of the 1920s looked about the right size, made about the right noise, looked fast enough to impress but were not

A race for touring cars, with hoods and electrics, tools and spares, and the stamina to see them through 24 hours of racing, continuous through the night and day, on utterly ordinary everyday town and country roads; that was what the Grand Prix d'Endurance was when it started at Le Mans in 1923.

so fast as to frighten. Better still, their designs lent themselves to ready adaptation as two-seater super-sports cars – indeed, until 1925 a riding mechanic had been obligatory company for the driver in a Grand Prix. Originally his duties had been many, the most important being to help with tyre changes; but as tyres grew better and more reliable (Pirelli began a long run of GP successes with the introduction of the P2 Alfa Romeo in 1924) his tasks were gradually reduced until he was doing little more than pump air into the fuel tank to maintain feed pressure, until finally he was no more than living ballast. When, as occasionally happened, he had the misfortune to become dead ballast, the need for his presence began to be questioned, and from 1925 he stayed where he belonged in the pits. For a while the cars still had to wear two-seater bodies, so no great engineering legerdemain was necessary to confect a really rabid roadgoing car by tacking lights and mudguards on to a thoroughbred thoroughgoing racer.

This was not really what people had in mind when the first of the great sports-car races were inaugurated. Indeed they were thought of as events for touring cars; but with the proliferation of new courses for Grand Prix machinery all over Europe that marked the early 1920s, it was inevitable that standards should rise and that higher levels of performance should be demanded of cars that were meant to be fit for use on the public highway.

As early as 1922 there had been an event known as the French Touring Car Grand Prix, run over the same course as the pukka race but contested by two-seaters, four-seaters, and heavyweight tourers, all of which had to be ballasted up to the weight of a full complement of adult passengers, and which were also handicapped according to their categories. However, what the French – whose logic could never be overcome by anything save their own patriotism – really wanted was a race that would try every aspect of a touring car, its lights and starter and hood and fuel consumption, its seating capacity and reliability, as well as its speed. What they wanted was a race such as the Tourist Trophy ought to have been but never was; what they got came for a while very close to that ideal, making its debut at 4 p.m. on 26 May 1923 as the Grand Prix d'Endurance des Vingt-Quatre Heures du Mans – the celebrated 24-hour race at Le Mans that has ever since enjoyed unquestioned and sometimes undeserved status as the greatest sports-car race in the calendar. The first race was won in rain and hail by a 3-litre Chenard-Walcker which covered 1373 miles by 4 p.m. on the following day. Perhaps the most propitious entry was the car that finished fifth, the 3-litre Bentley that was to win the race in 1924. Bentleys were to win again four times in a row from 1927, and the legend that surrounded them did much to confirm the fascination of the Le Mans race for British enthusiasts.

The race in turn did much for the reputation of Bentley, for the cars were never so consistently successful elsewhere. The Bentley 4-cylinder engine in a 3-litre and 4½-litre form was an amalgam of pre-war racing car practice, revealing distinct affinities with the big GP Peugeot and the 1914 Mercédès. The rest of the car looked like a fugitive from a locomotive factory, and here again the affinity was not likely to occasion any surprise, for it was to that trade that former public school boy Walter Owen Bentley was apprenticed, before going on to be a Brooklands enthusiast and a wartime naval lieutenant responsible for the most powerful rotary aero engines in regular and successful military service. Indeed, to ride in a 4½-litre Bentley was not unlike riding on the footplate of a steam locomotive, while feeling the pulsations of the big 4-cylinder engine which 'W.O.' himself described fondly as 'that bloody thump'.

Yet it was not entirely these romantic associations, nor the car's respectable speed and monumental reliability, that won the team such adulation: the lay English public, which was never terribly interested in motor sport, was more interested in the fabulous exploits of the team drivers, the Bentley Boys, who seemed to epitomize all that was hale and hearty in British amateurism. They included a champion jockey, a Harley Street doctor, an artist and writer who was notably kind to his cars, a stammering little bantam-brave baronet who was equally cruel to them, and a Jewish diamond merchant who kept the whole Bentley business afloat for as long as he could, and who was probably the fastest driver of the lot. When they were not racing, life for the Bentley Boys seemed to be one long round of wildly extravagant parties in Mayfair and Belgravia, keeping each other company in a fine froth of beer and badinage; but when they were racing for 'W.O.' and for England, they gave themselves body and soul. The cars were big, especially the Speed Six that was Woolf Barnato's favourite, and keeping them pressed up to the bit for 24 hours called for a pretty soulful application of the body. Dr. Benjafield used to speak with awe of Barnato's upper arm, which he described as being as thick as the Benjafield thigh – and since the doctor's proportions suggested a cross between a Suffolk Punch and a siege mortar, the Barnato bicep must have been a force with which to reckon. The same could be said of the whole Bentley team – but in 1930 their assembled might (three 6½-litre cars entered by the factory, and another three supercharged 4½-litre cars backed by Miss Dorothy Paget) had their work cut out to win. They feared but one opponent, a solitary Mercedes-Benz (the two pioneer German firms had amalgamated in 1926) driven by the long-serving Werner and the supremely gifted young Rudolf Caracciola. One Bentley after another was sent ahead to play the hare, forcing the pace in the hope of breaking the Mercedes-Benz; and by the early hours of the Sunday morning, they had achieved their object. It cost them dear; the strain broke four Bentleys of the six that were entered, but those

The Americans tried hard to win at Le Mans, and often came close. A Stutz was leading after $22\frac{1}{2}$ hours when it retired in 1928, but two Chryslers like this one (left) finished third and fourth that year and sixth and seventh in 1929. On both occasions a Bentley won . . . but the ladies had not come to see that?

that remained could tour around to finish comfortably first and second. That was the end for Bentleys at Le Mans, and the following year (1931) would be the end of the firm; but the beginning of that momentous battle of 1930, and all the glamour and tension of the traditional Le Mans start (the drivers had to run across the road and leap into their cars, which were lined up in echelon before the pits with their engines dead) was captured by one of the men best qualified to do it, Dr. Dudley Benjafield himself:

At long last the great day dawns; Saturday, June 21st, and it looks like being a scorcher; better that than wet, though a cloudless sky in the late afternoon makes the run down to Arnage pure Hell, as it is here that the direction of the road is due West and the last two hours before sunset, the light is very trying.

Shortly after three o'clock the cars are lined up in front of the pits in a staggered row, the engines are run for a few minutes to warm them up, switched off and the hard racing plugs are substituted for the softer road ones and once more the engine is started to make sure that all the new plugs are firing, and after two or three bursts up to two five she is once more switched off and covered up with an old rug. With fifteen minutes to go, Babe Barnato (for the second year in succession) and Tim Birkin, last year's winners, with a couple of marshals in the back with a large yellow flag, set off round the circuit on "The Lap of Honour", to declare it closed to the public and open for racing. And now with five minutes to go everyone except the opening drivers are herded off the road by the officials. Glen Kidston, Frank Clement and Sammy Davis are opening with the sixes, whilst Tim Birkin and Ramponi are opening with the Hon. Dorothy Paget S/C $4\frac{1}{2}$-litres.

Titans: the lone Mercedes-Benz battles with one of the Bentley team ('the winning Speed Six') at Le Mans in 1930.

Caracciola is starting with the Mercédès and as the largest car in the race has pride of place at the head of the line. At flag fall he takes full advantage of this position and the long, low, white car streaks away with the supercharger screaming, closely followed by Kidston and Davis, and then a pack of cars which included Tim Birkin with No. 9 and Ramponi with No. 8. Only one car is left on the line, the 6-cylinder B.N.C. which had been pushed into its place in feverish haste a few minutes before the start and which, now that the flag had dropped, refused to respond, and had to be pushed off the stage, in dire disgrace, while the Grand Prix d'Endurance is yet only five minutes old.

Owing to the narrow road to Pontlieu and the two bends on the Rue de Circuit, little passing can be done until they come to the Hunaudieres stretch, but once this broad straight stretch is reached No. 9 Bentley goes through the mob like a knife through cheese, so that by the time Mulsanne is reached, the Mercédès is still in the lead, but Glen and Tim are on his tail. Immediately after the bend, Birkin forges ahead of Kidston, so that when they come into view of the expectant crowds in the grand stands, the low-built, white Mercédès, with its supercharger whining shrilly, is well in the lead. Birkin and Kidston following in close formation, Davis somewhat detached but well within striking distance, ready and anxious to take up the running, should anything go wrong with the leaders. Further reserves are close at hand as both Clement and Ramponi are only a few lengths astern. It is indeed an unequal battle, at any rate as far as numbers are concerned, but whatever the Mercédès firm may have lacked in quantity, they made up for in quality, both as regards machine and drivers. To appreciate the finer points of the really first-class driver, is almost impossible as a mere spectator, however well placed, and in my opinion, this can only be achieved by driving in the same race so that he may be kept under observation for a considerable distance. For instance, suppose one is lucky enough to have a seat in the grand stand, what does one see – merely car after car roaring past on full throttle whether he be a 750 c.c. M.G. or a 6,500 c.c. Speed Six Bentley. Certainly one would have to be

A faster Mercedes-Benz, the SSK, set new records in the 1931 Mille Miglia, driven by Caracciola.

built of stone not to be thrilled by the sight of Tim Birkin sitting bolt upright in the S/C 4½ roaring by at 120 mph at what appears to be about 6 inches astern of the long low white Mercédès, the shrill whine of whose supercharger monopolizes the sound waves. But as a mere spectator, one misses that superlative artistry possessed by few drivers and by none in greater degree than Caracciola, that enables him to pass another car on a fast left-hand bend on a wet road with anticamber. I actually saw him do this in the Tourist Trophy race, the year he won it as he had passed me shortly before . . .

With the passing of the Bentleys it was the turn of Alfa Romeo to dominate the Le Mans race for a few years, but in 1931 Caracciola in the Mercedes-Benz achieved something even more meritorious; he won the Mille Miglia, that race that promised to be the permanent preserve of Italian drivers on their home ground.

Created in 1927, the Mille Miglia was unquestionably the greatest motor race of all, and if it was unquestionably a race for sports cars the term had unquestionably to be understood in the most generous sense. A touring car could enter, for the meanest little family saloon would be welcome to participate; but outright victory could hardly fall to anything less than that blood-curdling artefact that was mentioned earlier; a two-seater Grand Prix car furnished with lights and mudguards. It would need all these provisions, for the race was as good as its name, covering a thousand miles of ordinary Italian roads. From Brescia to Rome and back again in a vast figure-of-eight crossing over the Apennines near Bologna, the route took in main roads and mountain passes, the long flat straights of the Tuscan plains, and the torturing succession of hairpins of the Futa and Raticosa passes, the total distance being equal to 1000 of the old Roman miles or *miglia* whence the race took its title. It was a return in principle to the great city-to-city races with which the history of the sport began, and like them it was run on a time basis with the cars starting

Most brilliant and colourful of Italian drivers, Tazio Nuvolari at Brooklands.

singly at intervals from the centre of Brescia and racing against the clock until they returned there.

The car that came home winner in 1927 truly came home, for the OM was built in Brescia; but thereafter the race became an Alfa Romeo preserve: the sensationally racey Milanese cars would have enjoyed an unbroken run of victories from 1928 to 1938 inclusive were it not for the interruption by Caracciola and Sebastian in their Mercedes-Benz in 1931. Caracciola had been doing amazing things with the big Merc, and was to do more. Winning in the wet in the Tourist Trophy was the first of his series of masterpieces, accomplished on the road circuit at Ards in Northern Ireland where the TT had been reconstituted as a sports-car handicap race in 1928. Caracciola had been doing well for Mercédès since he joined them, starting in 1924; but it was with the big Mercedes-Benz S series that he really demonstrated his worth, securing some outstanding wins on Germany's new and taxing Nürburgring in 1927 and 1928. Hillclimb championships and sports-car victories fell to him like grass to the scythe, but that Mille Miglia victory was outstanding, perhaps rivalled only by his extraordinary third place in the Monaco Grand Prix in 1929. That was the first year the event was held, on a short and twisty circuit that remains to this day the epitome of a round-the-houses race on genuine public roads all set about with manholes, masonry, and fever-trees. It was the sort of circuit on which Bugattis might be expected to shine, and so they did; it was not at all the sort of place where a walloping great $7\frac{1}{2}$-litre sports car might be judged appropriate; but there was nobody, not even Nuvolari, who could sit in judgement on Caracciola, who led the race for a while but had to defer to the Bugattis when pit stops for fuel and tyres set him more than two minutes in arrears.

Above : the Monza Alfa Romeo, very effective in 1930.   *Below : the T35 Bugatti, still effective in 1929.*

Like Ferrari in later years, Bugatti lost many races through a misguided choice of tyres. Those seen above served well at San Sebastian in 1926; by 1930, the problem was the age of the T35, but at Monaco (below) it won again. The 1½-litre Talbot (driven by Clemente Biondetti) leading Louis Chiron's T35 is a relic of the 1926/7 GP formula.

At Pau in 1930 the Bugattis even had to work pretty hard to stay in front of a Bentley – but the big British interloper was baronet Sir Henry ('Tim') Birkin's blown 4½-litre, and in a race of attrition it finished second.

The little principality of Monaco had become one of motor sport's focal points a good deal earlier than this. While the road-racing world was branching out in all directions, discovering natural road circuits in or around half the towns of Europe and building artificial ones adjacent to the other half, the get-there-at-all-costs brigade had been developing new events out of the old primordial reliability trials. Foremost of these was (and still is, in the public eye) the Monte Carlo Rally which was first held as long ago as 1911. In that year twenty-three cars set off for Monaco from Berlin, Brussels, Paris, and Vienna, in darkest mid-January, being required to average 15 mph and get there in a week. A Turcat-Méry driven by an apparently frost-proof Monsieur Henri Rougier was the outright winner, and the rally attracted so much popular acclaim that eighty-seven crews repeated the exercise the following year, starting from as far away as St. Petersburg. Unlike so many more pleasant things, this idea survived the Great War, and the rally was revived in 1924, with a starting point in Britain; in 1925 the organizers began the practice of giving bonus points for crews starting from the more difficult places, with a 50-mile mountain trial at the end of the rally to separate the goats from the sheep. The formula seemed a good one, for in those days merely to get to Monaco was difficult enough: not until 1931 did any competitor get to Monaco from Athens within the time allowed. On the other hand, so many cars were coming through the road sections unpenalized in the early 1930s that a rather artificial gymkhana-like driving test had to be conducted on the harbour front as a tie-decider, and

Saloons heading for Monte Carlo – 1928 top left, 1930 bottom left, and 1934 above.

this practice led to some wildly unsuitable cars triumphing because they had been designed or adapted for a good performance in this wiggle-woggle, it being assumed that anything decent on four wheels could manage the rest of the course if well driven. In other words the rally was ceasing to be suitable for the sensible touring cars for which it was intended; but not until after the World War was anything effective done about it.

Rallying was by no means the only distraction from the regular merry-go-round of road racing. Some people had always been attracted by the simple matter of driving faster in a straight line than anybody else. As early as 1899, Camille Jenatzy and the Comte de Chasseloup-Laubat had been competing for this honour in their electric cars, the former succeeding in raising the record above 100 kmh. The 100 mph mark was passed in 1904 by the Frenchman Rigolly in a Gobron-Brillié, but the biggest jump was made by the mighty 'Blitzen' Benz in which Victor Hémery reached nearly 126 mph in 1909. In the following year the American Barney Oldfield exceeded 131 mph in the same car, and that for the time being was that – not until 1922 did Kenelm Lee Guinness (whose initials became a trademark for spark plugs) raise the record a little higher in a Sunbeam. The 1920s were a period when record-breaking became more a business than a sport: manufacturers of oils, spark plugs, tyres, pistons and so on found it commercially worthwhile to pay good bonus money for the right to advertize their association with a successful attempt on the record, and the protagonists quickly learned the art of breaking the existing record by the smallest acceptable margin.

They had to budget very carefully, for the costs of building a special car and transporting it to one of the few suitable venues, the Pendine Sands of Wales or Daytona beach at Florida, were formidable. Many of the competing cars were therefore surprisingly crude affairs, cheaply flung together from lorry chassis and government surplus aero-engines. All through the 1920s the cars grew bigger and bigger and the increments smaller and smaller. The leading drivers were the Englishman Sir Henry Segrave, the Welshman J. G. Parry Thomas, and the Scotsman (later Sir) Malcolm Campbell, with occasional challengers from the U.S.A. The only American to be successful at this time was Ray Keech, driving the crudest monstrosity of them all, the White-Triplex with which he captured the record at 207·55 mph in 1928; but it was a terrible tragedy that his most deserving compatriot Frank Lockhart should have been killed in that same year while trying to capture the record in the only car of real technical merit to attempt it in a decade.

Lockhart was young, poor, almost illiterate and mechanically almost a genius, and he somehow persuaded the Stutz company to build him a tiny slim slipper-bodied car that would pierce the air like an unbuttoned rapier, a car that might exceed 225 mph under the impulsion of a highly supercharged 3-litre engine. For commercial reasons the car was christened the Black Hawk Stutz, and for technical reasons that were beyond contemporary American understanding of chassis dynamics the car crashed on Daytona beach, taking Lockhart with it. If only it had succeeded, as it deserved, the course of record-breaking history might have been changed, and the megalomania of succeeding years avoided, for the 400 bhp 16-cylinder engine that drove this razor-keen car so fast was in fact two straight-eight Miller engines linked side by side. As any American familiar with automobile racing will tell you, there is something very special about a Miller engine . . .

In America and especially among the racing fraternity around Los Angeles the reputation of Harry Armenius Miller is as high as a cat's back. This Harry A. Miller is a boy who works hard and soon has his own business so that when America goes into the Great War he is already making pistons and carburettors and a serious amount of money. He also gets involved with racing cars and remakes the engine of a GP Peugeot that Bob Burman has blown up. The engine goes better than the car and eventually Burman kills himself, but by this time Harry Armenius is busy building an aero-engine for Lincoln Beachey. It is a very good engine but the plane is not so good and Beachey kills himself. This looks bad but it does not look surprising to Harry Armenius, who is such a guy as might be thought strange on account of he admits to occult inspiration for his ideas which seem to come to him without any working out. It seems likewise that he is some kind of

Hill-climbing became more than a sport: in Britain and Europe, it became an art. Here are two famous venues: above, Shelsley Walsh, dominated for decades by Raymond Mays here driving a stripped 4½-litre Invicta; below, Mont Ventoux, where twin rear wheels give added traction to the 2½-litre Maserati in which the gifted 21-year-old American amateur Whitney Straight breaks Caracciola's record in 1933.

clairvoyant, being especially good at forecasting exactly where and when certain people will die. He is more surprised when he gets an order for half a dozen engines for planes and cars, and more surprised still when Barney Oldfield comes to tell him that he wants the same thing only even better. One way and another Harry Armenius Miller is doing good business as an engine maker, the only trouble being that he is not a practical engineer apart from which he is not a theoretical one either. Actually he is just a bunch of bright ideas waiting for somebody to make them work, and he gets himself assisted by one Leo Goossen who comes to him with a note from Chrysler saying he can do just that.

This Leo Goossen is one of those quiet-working characters who does not make much noise because everything he does is so good that no amount of noise-making will make it any better; and the engines he designs for Harry A over the years are so very good, and Harry sees to it that they are made so beautifully, that they go on and on for ever, lasting longer than Harry or the Duesenburg or Offenhauser or anybody else associated with them, just getting rejigged from time to time when somebody wants an engine that much bigger or that much smaller and with or without a supercharger. Harry himself has ideas to offer, some of which are his own and others of which come by such devious routes as around the blind side of Tommy Milton. The upshot of them all is that Goossen draws him a 2-litre straight-eight that is upstairs like the straight-eight Fiat and downstairs like Fort Knox, whereupon some angel gives Harry the bright idea of planting one of his carburettors alongside each of the eight cylinders. Harry does not have a dynamometer, and does not need one because he has lots of assorted lengths of inlet pipe, a stopwatch, and an oval track nearby, and so he pioneers the use of ram pipes ten years before they are invented by a tough English character called Freddie Dixon who is not only a clever mechanic but can also ride a Harley-Davidson down to the wheel nuts. After 1924 this does not matter, because in 1925 everybody has superchargers. Harry Armenius is included in this, but he has something else as well, an idea for front-wheel-drive that comes to him from the late Jimmy Murphy.

Of course there are front-drive racing cars in America before this: Barney Oldfield is doing very nicely thank you with a V4 Christie back in the days when Lancia was still trying to break out of the family soup business. Harry Miller does it better than Christie or anybody: he works out a De Dion front suspension like the one that everybody forgets from the 1890s and that Mercedes-Benz remembers in 1937 after which it always gets to be used somewhere – and suddenly the drivers at Indianapolis find that they can take the corners faster than ever so long as they keep the throttles open. They also discover that if they allow the throttles to close they can hardly take the corners at all. While they are learning this at 15,000 dollars a time, Goossen is working out a new engine for the 1½-litre Formula of 1926 that the Europeans forget works out at a singularly odd 91 cubic inches. This engine in the front-drive Miller chassis is the high point of Harry's achievement: it races under a multitude of titles including Duray-Miller and Packard Cable Special and it wins everything in sight. On a board track it sets a world closed-course record of 148 mph that stands for twenty-four years – and then along comes young

The 1934 Alpine Rally was made politically welcome by the Germans; the Hotchkiss on the hill showed that the French were still to be taken seriously. The English sought fun; forbidden to race on their roads, they resorted to their widest beaches (Southport was a favourite) and raced on the sands.

Frank Lockhart to get another 98 horsepower out of it, making 252 with what Goossen had already contrived, and he does a flying mile at 164 mph. He aims to do better and that is how he gets killed. Two years later Harry Miller gives up motor racing because he hopes to do better and that is how he goes bankrupt. Still, everybody remembers that it is a lovely 91 inch engine . . .

Europe too had some lovely engines in the years of the $1\frac{1}{2}$-litre Formula, which were effectively 1926 and 1927. Those were the years in which the French were able briefly to interrupt the autocratic rule of Italy. The fastest cars, if not always the most reliable (those were the Bugattis, which remained as successful as ever) were the Talbot-Darracq and the Delage, both of them low-slung straight-eights so full of roller bearings that a fellow might wonder where the fuel went. In fact, under the impulsion of a supercharger it went in and out with estimable efficiency, and these cars were very fast indeed. The Talbot was never very fast for very long, and in 1926 the Delage had to be stopped frequently so that its drivers could quench their roasted feet (the exhaust pipes passed much too close), but in 1927 the Delage was never beaten in any race that mattered. Indeed there was only one car that might have been faster, a 12-cylinder $1\frac{1}{2}$-litre Fiat that was the finest and fanciest piece of racing machinery ever built by them or up to that time by anybody else. It never raced against the Delage, appearing only once in a wet-weather race that was only one-tenth the length of a representative Grand Prix. The only real opposition came from a 2-litre P2 Alfa Romeo driven by the great Giuseppe Campari, whom Pietro Bordino left as though standing. It was Fiat's last race, and no car of comparable cleverness was to be seen racing in the next half dozen years.

After the demise of the $1\frac{1}{2}$-litre formula, an unwonted freedom from restrictions left the racing-oriented

The greatest of the European hillclimbs were staged on famous Alpine and Apennine passes, routes long enough to bring out the best in a good Grand Prix car. The apotheosis of the classical GP car was surely the monoposto Alfa Romeo, in which the factory driver Mario Tadini – so long as his Alfa was going uphill, as here on the Stelvio in 1935 – was even faster than Nuvolari.

manufacturers strangely unhappy, and for four years chaos reigned. Then in 1932 engineer Jano produced the P3 Alfa Romeo which, though no more than a restatement of established principles, was welcomed as the epitome of the Grand Prix car and was soon to prove itself the most successful of its kind. This was the car of such heroes as Nuvolari, Varzi and Chiron, and it was the last effective champion of the classical tradition against the onset of German modernity. To succeed in this car against the Germans as late as 1935 called for more than heroism, however; thereafter even Nuvolari could not do it again.

CHAPTER THREE

THE NATIONS RAGE SO FURIOUSLY

1935–1957

The Germans preached Strength through Joy, but practised Blitzkrieg by Technology; and their cars (which utterly dominated Grand Prix racing until the World War) inspired a new generation, a new morphology which endured to represent modernity as long as racing cars remained front-engined. Grands Prix became romantic rather than classical, but the great classics among the races enjoyed golden ages – especially Le Mans and the Mille Miglia, while the importance of rallying grew with the size of the Monte Carlo event.

When
Achille
Varzi disputed with Nazi
drivers at divers
events when the Alfas were red
as the faces at Monza and monster
Mercédès played Hades as ladies displayed ease abed
quoting from old German Lieder
Neubauer's chaps indicated each lapse
but his lips counted laps and the chronographs gaps
imparting the charting of speeder and slouch which
Manfred von Brauchitsch
the bold German leader
had led in the furious red of his helmet with lead in his throttlefoot
and fire in his tyres
hoping with glory to master an Aryan race
drifting in powerslide style

Like Nuvolari at Bari the wheels tore around and
the pits' white hopeful mechanics replaced them in haste
while Rosemeyer raced for the flag

The years from the beginning of 1934 to the outbreak of the World War in 1939 are important for the promotion of technology and the demotion of simple sporting motives which then took place, apparently irreversibly; but they are most memorable for being pervaded by an overriding spirit of nationalism, cultivated to a degree unmatched in motor sport before or since. It was a period in which German teams, bearing the insignia not only of Mercedes-Benz and Auto-Union but also of the swastika, established such a superiority in Grand Prix racing that all other opposition to them eventually disappeared, and all other branches of motor sport appeared by comparison to be amateurish if not downright trivial. There was in fact splendid sport to be had at the wheel of some spindly home-built hill-climb special on the Worcestershire slopes of Shelsley Walsh; there was superb racing to be seen in the Mille Miglia; there were wonderful cars to be admired at Le Mans. Nevertheless, the memory of motor racing in the latter 1930s is completely dominated by a new breed of machines surrounded by an aura of invincibility, an aura tended by unprecedented publicity campaigns such as we would now classify as 'public relations' but which we then described as 'propaganda'.

If Germany had lacked Goebbels it could have fallen back on Virgil: *iam nova progenies caelo demittitur alto*, a new race now descends from on high. They were intent on the display of wealth, power, and a rigorous focussing of every technological and human capability towards the aim of motor-racing perfection. They did not immediately succeed: Nuvolari's victory, at the wheel of an obsolescent Alfa Romeo in the German GP of 1935, stands as one of the great human achievements of motor-racing history. Such drama notwithstanding, the German campaign allowed their rivals no cause for long-term optimism; and after the expenditure of much money, much material, much effort, and some blood, the consolidation of new design principles confirmed this period as the beginning of a new technocratic era. Here were cars like none that had been seen before; far more powerful, very much faster, considerably more comfortable, and endowed with superior roadholding and traction. Even Alfa Romeo, who were now state-owned, could not rival them, for the racing departments of Daimler-Benz and Auto-Union were encouraged in their expenditure by extravagant underwriting from the German government which (probably rightly) saw international motor racing as a most effective medium in which to publicize the assumed technical and human superiority of the new Nationalist Socialist state.

Mannschaft und Meisterschaft: The Fuhrer has spoken. The 1934 Grand Prix formula shall and must be a measuring stick for German knowledge and German ability. That formula had been published by the sport's governing body in October 1932, and as usual it reflected a concern that neither the cars' speeds nor the cars themselves should get out of hand. The ultra-high-powered track cars – the *Bimotore*, the Type 54, and the *Sedici Cylindri* – built shortly before by Alfa Romeo, Bugatti and Maserati had been frighteningly fast and visibly incorrigible, and previous attempts to inhibit performance by limiting engine size had clearly failed, so it

was resolved to limit the weight of the cars. This might have led to designs of dangerous frailty, so to encourage reliability and robustness the races were each to cover at least 500 kilometres. The weight limit for the complete car (less driver, tyres and fluids) was to be 750 kilogrammes.

It had been supposed that this formula would produce well-balanced but modest machines not unlike the classic Type 51 Bugatti or Tipo B Alfa Romeo. What it actually produced were cars revolutionary in design, and flabbergasting in performance, thanks to new schools of chassis design, and new recognition of the contributions to be made by metallurgists and fuel chemists. Thus the new German cars both had engines very much larger than can have been within the expectations of the committee that formulated the regulations according to which they were constructed. Both of them enjoyed an excess of power even greater than the size of their engines might suggest, due to the refinement of their design. Both of them employed fully independent suspension of all four wheels, large hydraulic brakes, some semblance of bodily streamlining, and all the advantages of strength, stiffness, lightness, durability, and thermal stability, that could be conferred on a machine by engineers having at their disposal the most extravagant and sophisticated facilities.

Nevertheless both gave trouble, albeit in different ways. Auto-Union and Mercedes-Benz had each created a racing car that was, despite visible ancestry in each case, really like no other that had ever been seen before. Each of them was in several respects a bold contrast to the other. Each of them was characteristically German in its engineering style, but they were conceived, designed, and constructed, in different ways. The detail differences were too numerous to list, but all were subordinate to the principal contrast that in the Mercedes-Benz the engine was in front of the driver and in the Auto-Union it was behind him, the former car having been designed to enjoy a high polar moment of inertia, and the latter with quite the opposite intention.

In fact the whole situation was a study in polarities. While the German motor racing axis, whose poles were at Stuttgart and Chemnitz, produced new cars that in most respects were poles apart, their products were at least as strongly contrasted to the cars of Italy, now the only other significant competing nation and at the opposite pole of the new Fascist axis. As we have seen, the Alfa Romeo (and the Maserati, which must not yet be forgotten) were built along lines that had been laid down by Fiat in their then revolutionary cars of 1921–1923; and those dates were by no means insignificant in themselves. It is probably little more than coincidence that the rise of Italy and the decline of France in the fortunes of motor racing in general and Grand Prix racing in particular may effectively be traced to the year 1922 in which Mussolini became dictator of Italy and developed a foreign policy calculated to reduce the influence of France. Undoubtedly the Fascist government that he headed encouraged the Italian motor industry in its efforts to overthrow the old regime and to crown the alleged emancipation of the Italian people with laurels plucked in the field of motor sport, but it is doubtful whether this encouragement took any very substantial form in specie. When

Hitler, already a confirmed and knowledgeable motor racing enthusiast, came to power in Germany in 1933, his approach was somewhat different, as anticipated by Mussolini himself: *I should be pleased, I suppose, that Hitler has carried out a revolution on our lines. But they are Germans. So they will be ruining our idea.*

Opening the 1934 racing season with a great flourish but suffering repeated setbacks, the Germans could not be seen to have made a very great initial success of their revolution. For all their new ideas, they were not achieving lap speeds on the new circuits very much faster than the classical cars of the previous year; and this may in some measure excuse the decision of Alfa Romeo, Bugatti and Maserati to cling to their old ideas a little longer, hoping that straightforward development of them would keep their cars competitive. If they needed any excuse, the real one was a matter of simple economics. The fortunes of the Maserati company were founded on the economical design and modest production of racing cars and sports cars for sale to private customers, and they simply did not have the resources to compete with larger and wealthier organizations. For the rest of the decade, they were a spent force; and Bugatti, relying on a similar balance of accounts, had gone into the same decline. It is true that the Type 59 Bugatti, which will always deserve being remembered if only as the most surpassingly beautiful of racing cars, actually won the Belgian GP in 1934; but that was a race from which the German teams absented themselves, refusing to pay the exorbitant

Professionally purposeful 5.57-litre V12 Mercedes-Benz at Avus, 1937.   *Opposite: amateur's Bugattis (T35 above, T59 below) at Prescott.*

duties demanded by Belgian customs officials for admission across the border of the large quantities of special fuel that they brought with their cars.

If the crowds looked to anybody to beat the Germans when they were represented, it was to Tazio Nuvolari. This mercurial Italian, whose racing career started on motorcycles in 1920, was born in 1892 of a landowning family; and by selling some of his property in 1927 he was able to set up a private stable of Type 35 Bugattis, one of his team drivers being the great Achille Varzi who was for many years to be his sternest rival. The men were greatly contrasted: Varzi cold and calculating, always immaculate in his dress and in his driving, while Nuvolari was colourful, bizarre, mercurial in the cockpit and utterly original in his driving style. Sitting well back from the wheel, he flung his car sideways into a slide before each corner, slowing it by scrubbing the tyres rather than by using the brakes and then using the engine's power to complete the corner in the stable four-wheel drift that he is supposed to have invented. By 1930 he was thus abusing or exploiting the Pirelli tyres of the Alfa Romeo factory team, for whom he won the Mille Miglia and the Tourist Trophy that year in the elegant 6-cylinder 1750 sports car. In the following years his triumphs included repeated victories in the Targa Florio, the Mille Miglia, and Grands Prix galore, not forgetting wins in 1933 at Le Mans and in the TT in which latter he was driving (of all things!) an MG Magnette. When he came up against the Germans from 1934 onwards he was really on his mettle. His most famous victory against them was in the 1935 German GP on the Nürburgring, but there were some other virtuoso performances. In the 1934 Italian GP he drove a Maserati, finishing in fifth place with no brakes whatever:

mechanics had had to drain even the brake fluid to make the car light enough to pass the regulation weighbridge test during scrutineering, and they had forgotten to restore it afterwards! Again in 1936 Nuvolari beat the German cars in the Hungarian, Penya Rhin and Milano Grands Prix, but even more remarkable was his race at Livorno (a circuit he liked) against the Auto-Union team. He started in the latest 12-cylinder all-independent Alfa Romeo, but this ran into back-axle trouble on the first lap, so he took over the older 8-cylinder Alfa Romeo of his team-mate Pintacuda and set off after the Germans. One by one he passed them all and took the lead, pressing them so hard that their brakes (not relined since racing in the German GP a week earlier) began to fail; thereupon the Auto-Unions were passed by Brivio and Dreyfus, giving Alfa Romeo an unexpected clean sweep of the first three places.

These were exceptional results. More and more often it was the German cars that dominated the racing, and they had their exceptional drivers too. European enthusiasts flocked to see them racing, avidly read every newspaper report of their feats, and argued interminably about their rival merits.

The Auto-Union team was the more changeable, because the car was exceptionally difficult to drive and the search to find its master seemed never-ending. Initially the car was entrusted to Hans Stuck, famous across all Europe as the king of the mountains, the most successful hill-climb driver in the sport. He began in 1924, rapidly graduating to successively more special Austro-Daimler cars, with one of which he visited England in 1930 and set a new record for Shelsley Walsh. The following year he moved to Mercedes-Benz and continued to dominate the hills while enjoying some racing success as well. In the Auto-Union in 1934 he was tolerably successful but disappointing thereafter. In 1935 the team pursued fresh talent, looking particularly among racing motorcyclists and finding an outstanding one in young Bernd Rosemeyer. He had never driven any other racing car and for all he knew they were all like the formidable Auto-Union, which he flung around with great abandon. Once he had made his mark, which he did in his second race by challenging the great Caracciola, he was a national hero and the Auto-Union team relied on him (perhaps unfairly) to compensate for all the shortcomings of their cars – until he was killed during an attempt to recapture the flying kilometre record on the Frankfurt-Darmstadt Autobahn. The record had just been pushed up to 268 mph by Caracciola in a streamlined Mercedes-Benz, and in an ill-advised attempt to beat this on a gusty day in a similarly streamlined Auto-Union, Rosemeyer's career ended against a concrete bridge. That was in January 1938, when at last (under the provisions of a new racing formula which forced the rival firms both to make entirely new cars) Auto-Union had a machine that was competitive and not particularly difficult to drive. To replace Rosemeyer they engaged Nuvolari, who served them very well.

Hermann Lang, fastest pre-war GP driver; above, a 3-litre Delage, one of the faster pre-war sports cars.

Mercedes-Benz were no less well served by their team of drivers, which remained more stable. Unquestioned leader in the eyes of the management and of the public was Rudolph Caracciola, who had not only great gifts but also tremendous experience – and who had demonstrated in 1932, when he spent a season driving for Alfa Romeo, that he could outdrive Nuvolari on an equal car. Every one of his team-mates would have been glad to prove an ability to outdrive Caracciola, and not infrequently crossed swords with the team manager Alfred Neubauer – a dangerous thing to do, for the man was the strictest of disciplinarians – in attempts to do so. Luigi Fagioli was one of these, but what really irked the tremendously competent Italian was that he was sometimes expected to play second fiddle to another team mate who was much less experienced. This was Manfred von Brauchitsch, nephew of the famous fieldmarshal and hitherto a privateer who had only come to the fore in 1932. He was a rather uncompromising driver, proud and ferocious in his characteristic red helmet, inclined to drive furiously even if it meant an extra pitstop for fresh tyres – while the shrewd Caracciola would go by, driving with the unfailing smoothness and mechanical sympathy which made him unbeatable in the wet and economical in the dry. Neubauer engaged other drivers from time to time, such as the wiley Louis Chiron and the popular if less successful Geofredo Zehender; but it was by promoting the mechanic who tended Fagioli's car that at last he found a driver who could outpace all the others. This was Hermann Lang, who combined an intimate knowledge of the cars with motorcycle racing experience and tremendous spirit to become the fastest road-racing driver in the world by 1939.

Team manager Neubauer signals Manfred von Brauchitsch to go slower, since he leads Nuvolari by 30 seconds – and the 1935 German GP was won by Nuvolari.

Pit lane, Nurburgring, 1938: in comes a V12 Mercedes-Benz. Fuel boiling in the engine – bay heat often made restarting difficult.

There were other drivers, other cars, other races; but the German teams in the Grands Prix were the cynosure of all eyes. After the teething troubles of 1934 it was Mercedes-Benz, with their supercharged straight-eight giving 430 bhp from four litres, who were victorious nearly everywhere. In 1936 the tables were turned: the Mercedes-Benz engine was enlarged and uprated to as much as 494 bhp, but a new short chassis made the car very difficult to handle. Auto-Union, whose more lightly stressed V16 engine had grown from 5-litres and 375 bhp in 1935 to 6-litres and 520 bhp for 1936, enjoyed their best year ever, thanks in no small part to the virtuosity of the young Rosemeyer.

The 750 kg formula was due to expire at the end of 1936, but it was not until February of that year that the succeeding formula was finalized, and so the manufacturers were granted a remission of one year before it should take effect. Auto-Union accepted that their 1936 car would serve for another year while they prepared something new for 1938: it must have been a shock to their drivers . . .

It's no go the opposite lock, it's no go the corrections,
Loll in the back of a limousine and give the chauffeur directions.
Their blowers are driven by bevel gears, their axles swing from the centre,
Their driving seats are a foot from the ground, and only the brave may enter.

Ernst von Delius crested the rise, felt that he was flying,
Crossed the verge at hedgetop height and we knew that he was dying.
It's no go the Nürburgring, it's no go the censure,
Drive on your ear round the Karussell and draw a bow at a venture.

It's no go the powerslide, it's no go the steady,
All we want is a refilled tank and a set of tyres at the ready.
It's no go the starter's flag and letting the spin diminish,
It's no go the record lap and a glass of fizz at the finish,
It's no go the slipping clutch, it's no go the braking,
Sit on the grid in your linen hat and remember the orders you're taking.

But Mercedes-Benz, distressed by the behaviour of their 1936 car, had designed a new chassis for the anticipated new formula, and this was rapidly adapted to take an entirely new engine, larger than any they had previously thought feasible within the terms of the 750 kg formula. Once again it was a straight-eight, a direct inheritor of traditions established by Fiat in 1921, except that the cylinder head and valvegear was more reminiscent of the work of Ernest Henry. It was an amazing engine, extraordinarily powerful: it displaced no less than 5·66 litres but weighed only 494 lb, a mere 45 more than the original 3·4-litre engine of 1934; and before long it was giving 545 bhp on its basic testing fuel of petrol and benzol. For racing, a fuel rich in alcohol and laced with acetone, nitro-benzine and ether, raised the power output to 572 bhp and, with a special carburettor to exploit that fuel, the engine eventually gave 646 bhp, far more than any Grand Prix car before or since. It was power that could be used: the new chassis was better in all its details but especially in the rear suspension, where the independently swinging half axles had given way to a De Dion dead beam axle. Under the enthusiastic direction of the brilliant young engineer Rudolf Uhlenhaut, the 1937 Mercedes-Benz had a chassis which ensured dependable understeering stability, for Uhlenhaut could drive these cars at racing speeds and knew that there was enough power on tap to induce oversteer whenever the driver wanted it. This car was no less than a watershed in design: for another twenty years it would be offered the sincerest form of flattery as designers everywhere copied it, sometimes in its essentials and sometimes even in its appearance.

In 1937 it was supreme, with more usable performance than anything then known. Around the houses of Monaco it was geared for a maximum speed of 122 mph in fourth gear, second and third being almost identical so that the driver could take whichever came most readily to hand in that frenzied race of a thousand corners; for the long straights and frighteningly fast curves of Spa it was geared for a maximum speed of 200 mph; but as a general rule it was set up to reach 73 in bottom gear, 114 in second, 132 in third,

and 166 mph in fourth gear. In this form it could accelerate from standstill to 60 mph at an average rate of about 0·7g, with peak instantaneous rates considerably higher at some stage in this phase and not necessarily much lower even after the driver had changed up into second gear which would carry the car on to reach 100 mph in about ten seconds from the start. Such rates of acceleration were not matched in deceleration, for it was not then the practice of drivers to risk overheating fade and rapid wear of the brakes by hard usage: the normal practical rate of retardation was about 0·3g. In consequence these cars spent about one third of their racing time in being accelerated, about one third on the overrun, and the remaining third in braking, and the characteristic scream of the Mercedes-Benz supercharger combined with the deep roar of the exhaust to impress these phases upon the ears of the spectators, the car's periods of relative quietness being as eloquent as those when it was on full noise.

Rosemeyer fought valiantly for Auto-Union, and the rest of the team did their best; but it was to little avail. As part of the Nazi propaganda campaign the German teams travelled everywhere in imperial pomp, but the domination of racing by Mercedes-Benz in 1937 was no less imperious, and only very occasionally did capricious misfortune or valorous Rosemeyer frustrate their ambitions.

1938 brought a new formula, imposing engine limits of 3 litres if supercharged and $4\frac{1}{2}$ litres if not. Both Auto-Union and Mercedes-Benz built V12 engines to suit, and when Mercedes-Benz increased their power still further by adopting 2-stage supercharging (in which they were rapidly emulated by Auto-Union) the new cars became very nearly as fast as the 1937 machines, with Lang occasionally even faster in 1939. The Auto-Union, still rear-engined, now had a De Dion back axle and became much more controllable, and in the hands of Nuvolari it scored some wins, notably the last of the pre-war races at Beograd in Yugoslavia; but in general it was Mercedes-Benz who made the running, their only severe setback being the tragic loss of the gifted young English driver Richard Seaman from burns received in a crash on a wet corner at Spa.

That Yugoslavian race was peculiar in that it started six hours after the declaration of war on 3 September 1939. The last major European race to be held while the nations were technically at peace was the Swiss Grand Prix at Berne, and this was unusual in containing a class for cars of $1\frac{1}{2}$-litre displacement – among which a Type 158 Alfa Romeo driven by Dr. Giuseppe Farina lapped at 99·4 mph in practice (compared with Lang's best of 106·23) and finished sixth in the race itself. As at other times in the history of motor racing, an interest in voiturettes arises whenever Grand Prix cars (or their equivalents in the first decade of the sport) grow so large, so powerful, so fast, and so unreal, that they suffer some estrangement from the general public. This natural tendency was encouraged by the Italians towards the end of the 1930s; unable

to compete with the Germans on equal terms, they proposed a $1\frac{1}{2}$-litre engine limit for races held in their territory, and contrived to have this category recognized in some other countries too. Tripoli they considered within their domain, but they were careful to give the minimum possible notice that the Grand Prix there was to be run to Italian rules. They were hoping for a victory by one of the surprisingly fleet little Alfettas (long slim supercharged straight-eights, clearly derived from the unsuccessful 3-litre cars) or perhaps the new Maseratis which could produce good lap times with the aid of streamlined bodywork to suit the very fast Tripoli circuit. Their expectations were confounded, for Mercedes-Benz went to enormous trouble to build a pair of 2-stage supercharged $1\frac{1}{2}$-litre V8 cars essentially similar in every other respect to the reigning V12 3-litre, and these simply ran away with the race. It must have been the cruellest put-down in all racing, and also the most expensive.

Elsewhere voiturette racing had begun to flourish in the late 1930s. Richard Seaman had indeed made his reputation and attracted the attention of the Mercedes-Benz Rennleiter Herr Neubauer by racing a resuscitated 1927 $1\frac{1}{2}$-litre Delage with incredible success. There was no organization in Britain with the resources to field a competitive Grand Prix car, but a happy band of enthusiasts were beginning to drive in domestic events – and occasionally to participate in major international ones, from purely sporting

Highly supercharged, cleverly detailed, improbably fast: the racing single-seater Austin Seven.

motives – in a car called the ERA (for English Racing Automobiles) mechanically derived from the sporting Riley and built by a tiny company founded by Humphrey Cook and Raymond Mays. The latter already enjoyed some fame in Britain as the nation's leading hill-climb expert, devoting himself to this branch of the sport so wholly that he deserved to be ranked with the two other great hill-climb specialists of his generation, Hans Stuck (whom we have seen in the Auto-Union context) and the Italian Tadini who occasionally raced as a member of the Alfa Romeo team but could out-perform any of its members when the going was uphill.

Voiturettes or not, the crowds still flocked to see the Grands Prix, especially in Germany where crowds of a third of a million assembled each year around the seventeen and a half miles of corners and switchbacks which made the Nürburgring the most incomparably difficult and realistic road-racing circuit, even though it was not composed of public roads – this vast work had been completed between 1925 and 1927 at the instigation of the German government, not only to provide a testing ground and racing circuit for Germany's growing motor industry but also to give work to the unemployed. Only two circuits remained its superior, the Italian and Sicilian routes of the Mille Miglia and the Targa Florio, and by now both of

Jaray-streamlined 1939 Mille Miglia Fiat 1100.

these were sports-car events, the Sicilian race having been thus appropriated in 1936. Sports-car racing was much more to the taste of the British and French anyway, and there was no questioning its appeal to the Italians, and so the Germans were increasingly left to their own themes in the Grands Prix, while elsewhere the two-seaters realized a lively counterpoint. The British and French were at their best at Le Mans, where the former did consistently well in the $1\frac{1}{2}$-litre class with the handsome Aston Martin, outright victory usually resulting from a battle between the big French sports cars from Bugatti, Delage and Delahaye, though Alfa Romeo were always in contention. The British could build big sports cars (a $4\frac{1}{2}$-litre Lagonda had won at Le Mans in 1935 and a pair of V12s of the same make came close to doing so in 1939) but they generally tended to look like something that had escaped from Brooklands and had really been built for the bumps there. Among the smaller British sports cars, only two makes enjoyed an international reputation, Frazer Nash for their stirring performances in the Alpine Rally, and MG for the occasional blisteringly fast racer or record-breaker which stood out in bold contrast against a background of low-priced little runabouts that were more cosmetic than competitive.

All these sports cars and their contemporaries – Adler, Alta, Fiat, Georges Irat, Peugeot, Triumph and dozens more – were in their essentials pretty old-fashioned. As with the racing car, so with the sports car, it was once again the German industry that felt impelled to impart a new direction to the development of the motor car, and this time it was BMW who were the agents of change. They had introduced at the 1936 Berlin Motor Show their new Type 326 saloon, a car which in many respects (and particularly in its chassis, the suspension of which was not significantly bettered in a full-size saloon until 1958) set new standards for construction and behaviour. A sporting version of it was made in which Ernst Henne, famous for his record-breaking exploits on BMW motorcycles, won a race at the Nürburgring in that same year. This two-seater, with a tuned version of the ingenious and exceptionally efficient 2-litre 6-cylinder engine, went on sale in 1937 as the Type 328 and it immediately took charge of the 2-litre class in all respectable sports car races. From the Tourist Trophy at Donington to the Grand Prix at Bucharest, from the nocturnal mists of Le Mans to the sunbaked sands of the Tobruk-Benghazi-Tripoli desert race, the 328 BMW lent the utmost emphasis to its statement of what a modern sports car should be like.

It was smooth and quiet and comfortable, its very effective independent front suspension being complemented by a decently stiff tubular chassis which gave the curvaceous body a good foundation – this was not one of those ramshackle affairs in which one door would fall open and the other jam shut if the car were parked on sloping ground. It was also light, fast, had good brakes and, by the standards of its time, exceptional acceleration. If there had been a Mille Miglia in 1939 it might have set the cat among the pigeons in Italy even then; but that traditional preserve of Pirelli-shod Alfa Romeos (and others, for practically every class winner was Pirelli-shod in those days) was held again in 1940, albeit in a very different form.

An accident in the 1938 race had made the event unpopular with the government, but the Brescia Automobile Club organized a race on a triangular circuit based on their home town, and although technically it was called the Brescia GP they kept the old Mille Miglia name alive by using it as a sub-title. That noble anglophile Count Giovanni Lurani, a doctor of engineering and an amateur driver of tremendous experience and uncommon talent, made a point of turning out in his overalls emblazoned with the badge of the British Racing Drivers' Club to welcome and hobnob with the German drivers who had been entered in a team of BMWs. There were four of these cars, in three different body styles (standard, streamlined-open and streamlined-closed) and it was the coupé driven by Baron Huschke von Hanstein which won at an average speed of 103·5 mph, testifying to a maximum speed of about 125 mph and a power output of about 130 bhp – then quite extraordinary for an unsupercharged 2-litre engine. The Germans had made their point yet again; but what was perhaps of more interest to the Italians was the appearance in the

Above right: displaying the style that began to be called 'the four-wheeled drift' through the wooded Bremgarten, a Tipo 312 Alfa Romeo in the 1938 Swiss GP.

Below: building 'specials' was an English hobby; none was as brilliant as this, the Lightweight Special (making its debut at Prescott in 1938) built by George Dowson (driving) and Alex Issigonis. With a 70bhp supercharged Austin Seven engine, it was 587 lb of inspired engineering.

Italian enthusiasm knows no bounds: a Fiat 500 in the 1937 Mille Miglia.

race of a pair of open two-seaters, their 1½-litre straight-eight engines composed largely of stock Fiat parts. They were designed by Massimino, one of the old Fiat design team who had gone to Alfa Romeo and worked with the man who semi-independently controlled their racing team, Enzo Ferrari. One of them was driven by a young fellow called Alberto Ascari, no less than the son of the great Antonio whose death had been so lamented in 1925 when he was the leader of the Alfa Romeo team of P2 Grand Prix cars. The youngster did well while his car lasted, but neither specimen finished the race; what was significant was their presence, for these were the first of Ferrari's own cars. The date was 28 April 1940.

Four weeks later, Luigi Villoresi led home a team of Maseratis that filled first three places in a race called the Targa Florio. It was far from being a tour of Sicily, just a tour around a park in Palermo, and was a race for 1½-litre voiturettes as it had been for the last four years. Things were no longer the same, though there was some consistency in the fact that all these last four races were won by Maseratis, all on Pirelli tyres. Things had not been the same for some time: as we have seen, the Italians and all others had fallen back before the regimented onslaught of the newly inspired and materially encouraged German companies, and what had once been a great rivalry between nations now took other forms. The only real rivalry in motor racing was between compatriot teams – between Mercedes-Benz and Auto-Union (though the latter nearly withdrew in 1939), between Alfa Romeo and Maserati, and most healthily between Bugatti, Delage, Delahaye and Talbot, the last two occasionally entering stripped unsupercharged sports cars in occasional Grand Prix races in 1939 and even more occasionally faring better than might have been expected.

It was no better than they deserved, however: the general want of support and international interest was largely supplied by such lesser teams as the French and by individual amateur entrants driving whatever inadequate machines they could obtain; but the most general tendency was to decry the luxury, the professionalism and the quasi-military organization of those two German teams that were then supreme and virtually unchallenged. In his history of Rome's Decline and Fall, Edward Gibbon commented that *It is*

Porsche Abarth in the French Alps.

Below : Ferrari driver incredulous.

always easy as well as agreeable for inferior ranks of mankind to claim a merit from their contempt of that pomp and pleasure which fortune has placed beyond their reach. It was often poverty and ignorance that guarded the virtue of those who claimed to disdain the achievements of their conquerors – but with the World War the time had come to put the matter to a different kind of test, and when that was succeeded by a shocked and troubled peace in 1945 there was little question of the battles being continued under the guise of motor sport. It was enthusiasm that revived motor racing: no longer a vehicle for political propaganda nor yet for commercial, it was more than a mere sport; it was literally recreation.

Its form was largely determined by what was available, and this particularly influenced the new formula for Grand Prix racing that was agreed in February 1946 after the sport's international governing body had been re-formed. The Alfettas were still in existence, there were plenty of little Maseratis about, some ERAs and Talbots; and from the performances they had demonstrated before the war it seemed that some viable racing could be expected if supercharged $1\frac{1}{2}$-litre machines were pitted against unsupercharged $4\frac{1}{2}$-litre cars which, though slower, were much less thirsty of fuel and might therefore be competitive if races were long enough to force the blown cars to stop for replenishment.

It worked well enough, but against such opposition as existed the Alfa Romeos were so easily able to prevail that the Italian firm felt justified in withdrawing from racing in 1949 in order to save money that, had it been spent on a racing programme for that year, could hardly have caused any more to be proven than had been already. As it happened, this abstention coincided with the first appearance of a Grand Prix Ferrari that could be taken seriously. There had been an earlier Ferrari in this class, a curious little V12 which appeared in 1948 and showed itself to be an underpowered oversteering miniaturized monstrosity with which the best of drivers could achieve little. The new Ferrari which appeared in time for the Italian GP at Monza in the September of 1949 was altogether better, and with it Alberto Ascari (by now one of the very best of drivers) made the most of 305 bhp and improved roadholding to win convincingly. Many new comets were swimming into our ken, but of all of them the Ferrari promised to shed the strongest and longest light. The man responsible for it had supervized the design of the Alfettas, had managed the Alfa Romeo racing team before that, had been a driver of distinction before even that. In 1919 he had been the first driver away in the Targa Florio that revived motor sport after the Great War, and now here he was injecting fresh life into the sport after an even greater. In 1949 his beautiful little unblown V12 sports car – a 2-litre jewel set off to perfection in a *barchetta* body with which Superleggera Touring inspired a whole generation of two-seaters – won the first post-war race at Le Mans, and scored the second of six successive

Not just another Shelsley Special (though that was how it started), the very successful Freikaiserwagen inspired a whole generation of British rear-engined single-seaters. The mock-Teutonic name came from the names of its creators Joe Fry and Dick Caesar.

victories in the Mille Miglia. That greatest of all road races had been revived in 1947, when it was won by a driver who made the race his speciality (he won it four times altogether), Clemente Biondetti, driving the same type of Alfa Romeo as he had used to win it in 1938.

Old names and associations were being revived everywhere. The winner of the first post-war Monte Carlo Rally in 1949 was the Frenchman Trevoux driving a Hotchkiss like the one with which he had tied for first place in 1939. A Hotchkiss was to win again in 1950, by which time the event was assuming unprecedented popularity and importance. The number of entries grew to reflect this, reaching a record 440 in 1953, while the revision of the route to incorporate a longer common route for all starters reduced the importance of the correct choice of starting place, and a tightening of the eligibility rules restricted the rally to genuine production touring cars. The British began to take an enormous interest, Sidney Allard starting from Glasgow in 1952 in a car of his own manufacture to realize the first British victory since 1931, when the winning car was an Invicta driven by Donald Healey – since 1946 another manufacturer in his own right. The Allard car, which had grown out of the one-day sporting trials that were a peculiarly English and exceptionally sporting form of competition, had a Ford engine; and in 1953 it was a Ford saloon that won. The Ford team manager was Ken Wharton, a man who certainly had relevant background experience: driving a Ford saloon in the 1952 event, he slid off the road while following the tracks of another car. The Ford flew out into space, crashed down the roadside ravine and landed on top of a Citroën. Wharton sought to apologize to its French driver, who dismissed his apologies with the utmost sympathy: the Citroën, he observed, was on top of a Renault.

Minor English trendsetters in 1939: ERAs at Crystal Palace, Allard (inset), and Alta at Brooklands.

Twin rear tyres gave extra grip. One of the worst places to lose it would be on entering the last right-hander of Prescott hill, opposite. Denis Poore also used them on his modified Tipo 308 Alfa Romeo up Rest-and-be-Thankful in Scotland.

It was another pre-war star, the Monegasque racing driver Louis Chiron, who won the Monte in 1954, and several of the great pre-war drivers remained in contention in all forms of competition in the early post-war years – three of the greatest, Count Carlo Felice Trossi, Achille Varzi, and Jean-Pierre Wimille, being members of the Alfa-Romeo GP team, though they were all dead by the time it returned to the fray in 1950. Others like Lang and Caracciola had passed their prime, while Nuvolari had kept his skill but not his health. Nevertheless the most influential of all the pre-war stars was the Shelsley Walsh record-holder Raymond Mays – not because of his driving, but because of his missionary zeal.

Mays had seen an ambition partially fulfilled when the need for an English racing automobile was met by the ERA. That operation, of which he had been the founder, had been a modest one; but there was nothing modest about his post-war ambition, which was to see a British racing motor that could take on and beat the best Grand Prix machinery in the world. All his time and efforts were devoted to this ideal, in pursuit of which he went soliciting help from every imaginable quarter of British industry. With their help, the former ERA designer Peter Berthon concocted an elaborate design introducing all manner of unfamiliar technologies; and on paper the BRM, which showed up in Grand Prix racing for the first time in 1950, should have outpeformed the Ferrari, the Alfa Romeo, and indeed anything else that might have offered itself for comparison, pre-war Germans included. It was a design in which nothing but incompetent workmanship and bad management had been allowed to stand in the way of theory, in which a chassis little more advanced in concept than that of Berthon's 1939 E Type ERA (and tantamount to a 1938 Mercedes-Benz with Auto-Union front suspension) carried an engine intended to have as many cylinders, as much

1939 Mercedes-Benz accelerates at Reims: 80 mph in bottom gear, 98 in 2nd, 134 in 3rd, 156 in 4th, about 190 in top ...

piston area, and as little frontal area, as feasible, and to operate at crankshaft rates and boost pressures perhaps even higher than had been thought possible. Alas, the more elaborate the concoction, the greater is the danger of too many crooks spoiling the broth: the co-operative nature of the BRM venture brought with it too much dissension and division. The car raced seldom, and a deplorable period of failures to finish or even to start made it the object of almost universal ridicule. Much of the derision was deserved, but little of it by Mays himself. Why then should he be accounted so important a figure in his time? It was because, in order to persuade the BRM's supporters of the importance of their aid, he had to persuade them of the importance of motor racing itself; and this message was taken up and relayed by each of them, growing rapidly into a crusade that swept England, not only in the veneered halls of commerce and the grubby corridors of industry, nor even only in the specialist motoring press, but in the popular media too. The national newspapers began to take an interest in a sport that they had previously dismissed as the preserve of monied triflers, for by now the nation's manhood (or such of it as had been fortunate enough to return from the war) had acquired a familiarity with mechanical transport that had played a vital part in their military service, and now they were willing and eager to derive entertainment from it. Most vociferous of those newspaper campaigners was the *Daily Express*, which sponsored a series of important race meetings – notably at Silverstone, one of the many wartime airfields that, being now superfluous to military requirements, were being converted into motor-racing circuits to which the crowds thronged as never before.

Le Mans: breaking into the light, braking into the darkness, the fastest cars maybe 90 mph faster than the slowest.

It was a new crowd, a different crowd, avid to learn. Somebody had asked the sports editor of one of the motoring papers what one should wear when going to a motor race: *Anything*, he was told, *so long as it's well cut*. That editor was already living in the past; in another decade the correct answer would have been perhaps anything so long as it was *not* well cut. The motor race had ceased to be a social occasion, and was on its way to becoming a spectacle and a shop window for the motor industry. Those British crowds could not yet hope to see a British car supreme or even competitive in Grand Prix racing, but in the lower echelons of the sport there was a good deal of patriotic satisfaction to be found in the success of British sports cars. Aston Martin in particular had been doing impressive things in long-distance sports-car races, but the occasion that offered the British most hope for the future was perhaps the *Daily Express* meeting at Silverstone in 1949, when the one-hour race for production cars was a walk-over for the XK 120 Jaguar, a new two-seater of ravishing looks and astonishing speed. Jaguar were building the two-seater in a limited series, using it to prove a new engine intended for saloons; so tumultuous was its welcome that the XK 120 went into full-scale production shortly afterwards, setting new standards for performance, looks, comfort, and sheer accessibility, that no manufacturer of traditionally respected sports cars could afford to ignore. In 1950 and 1951 it dominated the Alpine Trial, and in the latter year it won the Marathon de la Route, the longest, fastest and toughest rally of them all.

The event had a history going back to 1931 when it was staged over a route of 2800 miles from Liège to Rome and back again. It was a non-stop event, as much a race of attrition through mechanical or human fatigue as anything calling itself a rally could be, and in the 1930s the most successful competing make was the Bugatti – though it should be remarked that the 1939 event saw one of these cars joint winner with the Hotchkiss of Trevoux, star of the Monte Carlo rally. Revived in 1950, the Liège-Rome-Liège was made tougher. The clerk of the course, Monsieur Garot, said that the ideal Marathon should have just one finisher; and by 1952 the ideal was in sight, only 24 of the 116 starters returning to Liège in the time allowed. So tough did the rally become in subsequent years that it had to be diverted into Yugoslavia and Bulgaria in search of roads that could be used at the speeds anticipated without causing riots among the local populace. Thus the rally became the Liège-Sofia-Liège until eventually in 1965 even the Yugoslavs could take no more.

That was a long time later, and even by then the Marathon had failed to make much impression on the general public, no matter how greatly it was respected by rally drivers. The great sports-car event of the year was always the 24 hours race at Le Mans, attracting such attention that Jaguar felt justified in building cars especially for it. Thus the Jaguar C-type, first of a long line of sports-racing two-seaters that were no less superb for being so single-minded in concept, began a run of Le Mans successes that, continuing with successively refined models in 1953, 1955, 1956 and 1957, gave the British as much cause for pride as the very similar run of victories achieved by Bentley a quarter of a century earlier.

A manufacturer's championship grew out of the major sports-car long-distance races of which Le Mans remained the most important; but this championship never attracted the public interest to anything like the same extent as the world championship of drivers that was instituted in 1950, and was awarded on the basis of performances in the major Grand Prix races of each year. It was one of the most far-reaching developments ever to affect motor-racing, for as it grew to matter more and more, so motor-racing became less a contest between machines, more a contest between men. Protagoras, to whose 2000-year-old wisdom we have had occasion to refer earlier, was proving himself right again.

The measure of all things as far as Grand Prix cars was concerned remained the Alfeta, which in 1950 carried Giuseppe 'Nino' Farina to the first world championship. It was no longer having so easy a time of it: in previous years the Alfa Romeo team could afford almost to tour around in comfortable line-ahead, taking their corners cautiously and swamping with sheer speed on the straights any car that might have rivalled them in the bends. In 1950, however, Ferrari was beginning to dent their authority: with the aid of a brilliant new designer, Aurelio Lampredi, he produced a new unsupercharged car; and by the end of that year, when the displacement of its V12 engine had reached the full permitted 4½ litres, it had become clear

that the new Ferrari could challenge the Alfa Romeo in speed as well as outlasting it in autonomy. Only by dint of uprating and redesigning the Type 158 so much that it justified a new type number, 159, could Alfa Romeo keep their cars in front in the races of 1951; and even then they could only do so by accepting the penalty of a fuel consumption which, at about one and a half miles per gallon, was twice as heavy as what had seemed outrageous in the 1939 3-litre Mercedes-Benz and three times as bad as the most powerful of them all, the 1937 5·66-litre Mercedes-Benz.

It was to this pretty pass that we had been brought by the introduction of engine capacity limits in the years before the Great War when motor racing was still young; and it was to this level of despair that the classical supercharged straight-eight racing engine had been brought from its exciting beginnings in the

Fiat of 1923. *Mene mene tekel upharsin* – the balance of $1\frac{1}{2}$ litres blown against $4\frac{1}{2}$ litres unblown had weighed the Alfa Romeo against the Ferrari and found the former wanting when, in one of the greatest races in the history of the sport, the Argentinian driver Froilan Gonzales at the wheel of a Ferrari outdrove his compatriot Juan Manuel Fangio in an Alfa Romeo to win the British Grand Prix at Silverstone in 1951. Ferrari were to beat Alfa Romeo twice more that year, in the German and Italian Grands Prix, and it marked the end of more than the Alfetta. The reign of the supercharged engine was over.

There had been hopes that others might step into the breach vacated by Alfa Romeo when they retired from racing at the end of the 1951 season. However, all hopes of new blood in Formula 1 racing were dealt a fatal blow when in October of that year it was announced that the then current Formula 1 and Formula 2

Fangio, above in the 1956 Lancia-Ferrari, did not take part in the 1951 Pescara GP, so he stood by the roadside (one could, in those days) and waved down his fellow Argentinian Froilan Gonzales whom he judged to be driving the 4½-litre Ferrari needlessly fast (opposite, top). Ferrari's most gifted driver that year was Alberto Ascari, seen below ahead of a Gordini in the Italian GP at Monza.

rules would remain valid for only two more years, pending the introduction of a new Formula 1 which would permit unsupercharged engines of 2·5 litres displacement and supercharged ones of only 750 cc. Grand Prix racing simply fell apart then: nobody was going to spend money building and developing a new racing car that would be useless in two years time, and in the absence of any effective opposition to the new 4½-litre Ferrari (in particular, the failure of the BRM to live up to its promise), no race organizer was interested in staging any events for current Formula 1 cars. So once again everybody fell back on the voiturette class, the Formula 2 as it was now known, for unsupercharged 2-litre cars. In these, Ferrari and

The 500cc class offered relatively cheap single-seater racing to English enthusiasts in the late 1940s and early 1950s. Putting a 1000cc JAP V-twin in a Cooper chassis made it a prodigious sprint and hillclimb car, and confirmed the potential of the rear-engined layout (opposite). The 1951 Kieft was a more subtle design in which Stirling Moss (giving it a sensational debut at Goodwood, above) displayed his own potential.

Maserati kept the names of the Grands Prix alive for a couple of years, with intermittent and unconvincing support from the likes of Gordini, Cooper, and Connaught.

None of these was a real thoroughbred racer. Each had evolved by the adaptation of components from production cars, the French tuner Amedée Gordini basing his work on what was available from Simca. Most interesting and most portentous of this Formula 2 supporting cast was undoubtedly the Cooper, the product of a firm which was then in the transitional stage from infancy to maturity but was still very much a shoestring operation. Its origins lay in the British Formula 3 category, which grew up out of the idea of some Bristol enthusiasts that cheap motor racing might be enjoyed with tiny single-seater cars that were limited to engines of 500 c.c. capacity and motorcycle origin. This idea spread rapidly in the late 1940s and early 1950s, a period when the great wave of new enthusiasm for motor sport was sweeping across Britain, when you could hardly visit a garage without there discovering some fellow who thought that anybody could put together such a car and that he in particular could prove himself a great racing driver in one. So successful was the original Cooper (its chassis was composed of the front ends of two Fiat Topolini) that a demand for replicas grew, and thus the Cooper Car Company became racing car manufacturers. Enlarging their sights to build front-engined sports cars as well as the tiny rear-engined 500 single-seaters, they found that they had the makings of a Formula 2 car, still with the same crude independent suspension but very light in weight and cheap to buy and maintain. Humble though they were, these cars set many great drivers on the way to fame: Stirling Moss first made his reputation in Formula 3, Mike Hawthorn in a Formula 2 Cooper after some impressive drives in club events in a pre-war Riley. In Hawthorn's case, promotion from the ranks was almost instantaneous: he made his Cooper debut in 1952 at Easter, and in the summer of the following year he won the French Grand Prix in a factory-entered Ferrari. Of course it was only a Formula 2 Grand Prix, but the fact that Hawthorn won against the opposition of no less a driver than Fangio, who had been world champion in 1951 in an Alfa Romeo, confirmed his ability and his place in the Ferrari team; but

Old oil drums marked the inside of the Silverstone track for the Grand Prix in 1954, when Fangio's streamlined Mercedes-Benz skittled several of them.

when the lists were entered for 1954, the first year of the new Formula 1, that was perhaps not the best team in which to be.

The temporary decline of the Formula 1 car after 1951 may have made Grand Prix racing somewhat dull for a while, but it left a useful interim period of two years during which designers could debate with more than usual care how best to match their skills to the demands of the new formula. There had been other times in history where a similar hiatus had done similar good; the years 1909 to 1911 inclusive and 1928 to 1933 were both periods when Grand Prix racing, although nominally continuing, did so in a state of suspended animation, and those periods were followed by years in which new theories were stated with great conviction and demonstrated with no less emphasis. It was 1912 that gave the world the remarkable new Peugeot, 1934 which produced the no less remarkable Auto-Union and Mercedes-Benz. Now in 1954 Ferrari and Maserati had nothing on the stocks that was not a predictable extrapolation of their Formula 2 cars, with which they had been so busily engaged in keeping Grand Prix racing alive in the preceding two years; but other serious contenders were forthcoming whose work was original, unexpected, and interesting, and in fact the subsequent years were to be a golden age in Grand Prix racing, great drivers fighting for their laurels in cars of greater technical variety than had been seen in thirty years.

About the only feature that all the leading contenders had in common was that they were unsupercharged. In fact the only supercharged car ever fielded under this formula was a modest little machine entered by Taraschi in the Rome Grand Prix of 1954: this was the Giaur, its engine developed from a production Fiat, its chassis relying on Fiat components, the whole thing tiny, light, ineffectual, and doubtless tremendous fun. Of the cars that were to be taken seriously in 1954, two (the 4-cylinder Ferrari and the 6-cylinder Maserati) were of traditional form, and the other two (the straight-eight Mercedes-Benz and the V8 Lancia) were full of challenges to convention.

By far the boldest challenge to received dogma was offered by the Mercedes-Benz which was revealed at

The cars rolled out to the start of the Italian GP at Monza in 1958 include the last front-engined GP Lotus and the first disc-braked GP Ferrari.

Reims for the French Grand Prix. Its coming had been expected, its importance was accepted as axiomatic, but still its originality and complexity took everybody by surprise. Its engine, which lay on its side, had no carburettors, fuel being injected directly into the eight forged-steel cylinders; nor had it any valve springs, closure as well as opening of the valves being positively effected by supplementary cams. Its chassis, based upon a proper spaceframe of small-diameter tubing, did not have the by now obligatory De Dion axle that Mercedes-Benz themselves had revived in 1937, but instead a geometrical refinement of the swinging half-axle employing dead half-axle beams pivoted very low beneath the final drive. The brakes were inboard not only at the rear but also at the front, where the space available allowed drums of immense width to be accommodated. Detail refinements abounded everywhere, in the springing, the fuel system, and the uncompromising pursuit of perfection in the making of virtually every component. Yet however shocking these features might seem to the preponderantly conservative denizens of the motor-racing world, they were scarcely as shocking as the bodywork, which was an all-enclosing streamlined shell that would obviously pay dividends on the long straight roads which made up the very fast Reims circuit. Despite hectic efforts by the drivers of the Italian cars, most of which fell back in overstressed disorder, it was the

Moss, Maserati, Monza – in 1956, when he drove regularly
for Maserati, Moss won the Italian GP in resounding
style. He had developed a powered-drift technique which
took the car through fast bends with the tail out, the
steering on opposite lock, and all four Pirelli Stelvio tyres
leaving long black streaks on the track – especially the back
ones, which were kept on the verge of spinning.

German ones which dominated the race as they had the practice. The fact that the lap times they achieved were only faster than their rivals' by the narrowest of margins merely showed that the cars were driven as circumspectly as befits a first outing: the two Mercedes-Benz cars had exploited a sprinting bottom gear in their 5-speed transmissions (at a time when all but Gordini made do with four) to establish a substantial lead before the first corner, and thereafter they were never seriously challenged.

The boot was on the other foot at their next race, at Silverstone for the British Grand Prix. They simply could offer no challenge to the Italian opposition, discovering that their aerodynamic bodywork imposed gross handling deficiencies on the circuit's wet medium-speed corners. Disgraced and embarrassed, the German team went home to think again, and decided to sacrifice the 20% reduction in aerodynamic drag offered by the original streamlined body in exchange for the lightness, compactness, low frontal area, and good visibility for the driver, offered by a more conventional slipper-type body wrapped tightly around the very wide frame. In this form they appeared at the Nürburgring, where Fangio at last improved on the lap record that had been set by one of the 1939 cars, lending further support to the suggestion (based on his record practice lap in the dry at Silverstone a month earlier) that this new Mercedes-Benz was probably the fastest road-racing car the world had yet seen. This proposition was challenged at Monza, where the Maserati of Stirling Moss held a comfortable 20-second lead until an oil pipe broke, leaving a faintly embarrassing victory to Mercedes-Benz. That embarrassment was aggravated at Barcelona a month later, when they suffered defeat at the hands of Ferrari in the race and humiliation at the hands of Lancia in practice.

Only the second new car to be built to the new formula, the Lancia had been a long time coming, but its excellent performance and refreshing design made the wait seem worthwhile. It was nothing like the German cars, but it was nothing like the Italians either: it had a V8 engine stressed to act as part of the chassis, it had outboard pontoons or panniers serving as fairings to fill what would otherwise have been an area of turbulent air between the front and rear wheels, at the same time constituting fuel tanks – and these pontoons contributed to a very short and squat appearance that hinted at very responsive, even twitchy, handling.

In this it contrasted strongly with the Mercedes-Benz; but during the winter of 1954 to 1955 the German engineers revized their attitudes to this and completely altered the character of the car. The engine was given scheduled development which brought its power up steadily, but the most significant thing that happened that winter was that Engineer Rudolph Uhlenhaut, the designer responsible for the car,

*Porsche Spyders await the start of a Swiss hill-climb.
The competition Porsche of the 1950s grew much more
elaborate mechanically than production models, but to
good purpose; racing successes came thick and fast,
though it was not until 1959 that Porsche was able to win
the European Mountain Championship.*

dismissed the earlier theory of directional stability characterized by a good deal of dynamic understeer which he had introduced in the 1937 cars, and which all other racing car constructors (except Lancia) accepted. For the 1955 season he went further, introducing different versions of the chassis with three different lengths of wheelbase, sometimes with the front brakes outboard instead of inboard, sometimes with the engine set a couple of inches further forward. For the first time some effort was being made to provide a variation in the setting-up of chassis and suspension to suit the handling demands of differing circuits and differing drivers; and this was eventually to lead to the universally adjustable suspension that has been an enduring feature of racing cars since 1960.

The immediate effect was that, whereas in 1954 the Mercedes-Benz was twice defeated, in 1955 it only happened once – at Monaco, where failure in the complex valvegear could not unreasonably be blamed on the drivers, all of whom exceeded the rev limit they had been given. In all the other Grands Prix of the season, the German team was unbeatable: led by Fangio, who was by now recognized as the greatest driver of all, and with Stirling Moss providing the best possible support as their No. 2 driver, the silver cars ran away from the field time and time again.

In sports-car racing, too, the Mercedes-Benz team was almost invincible. For this category they fielded a 3-litre version of the car in a suitably streamlined two-seater body; and in this Moss, who freely conceded that Fangio could outdrive him in the Grand Prix cars, was by no means subordinate to the Argentinian world champion. In what was the finest performance of his career to date, and one of the most memorable in the history of the event, he won the Mille Miglia at record speed, averaging nearly 98 mph. With him as passenger was the distinguished journalist Denis Jenkinson (who, earlier in his career, had been passenger to the world sidecar-racing champion Eric Oliver) communicating pace notes to him so that he should know the nature of every corner or other hazard as he approached it. This was something entirely new, having been worked out by the pair in the course of assiduous practice during the months before the race, and it set an example that was to revolutionize rallying, where the functions of the navigator had for some time been in question.

The Mille Miglia was unquestionably the greatest Mercedes-Benz triumph of 1955, but in that year Moss in the sports-car version also won the Targa Florio and the Tourist Trophy. The latter was run at Dundrod in Northern Ireland, where a multiple accident aroused such hostility to the race that it was once again left homeless. Far more serious was the accident that occurred at Le Mans while Fangio's Mercedes-Benz and Hawthorn's Jaguar were engaged in a fierce battle for the lead. The cars immediately involved in the mishap

The Lancia-Ferrari team in the Nurburgring pits before the 1956 German GP.

were Hawthorn's Jaguar, Macklin's Austin Healey, and another Mercedes-Benz driven as a guest by the veteran Frenchman Levegh. Coming up very fast behind the two Englishmen who were engaged in mutual avoidance in front of the pits, the Frenchman was unable to avoid hitting the Austin Healey, whereupon his Mercedes-Benz became airborne and was deflected into the crowd opposite the pits, where it exploded and broke up: Pierre Levegh was killed, and so were more than eighty spectators. It was the worst disaster in the history of motor sport, more horrifying in its single sudden shock than all the several tragedies of the infamous Paris-Madrid race of 1903. The public outcry was understandably tremendous, and outraged governments everywhere reacted instinctively by banning all motor racing forthwith – sometimes temporarily, sometimes (as in the case of the Swiss, who had been seeking an excuse for many years) permanently. The repercussions have never completely died away. Any hope that they might was dashed by

Above : Castellotti (Ferrari) wins the 1956 Mille Miglia. The car behind is Cabianca's Osca.
Below : servicing en route for the Mercedes-Benz 300SL in the 1952 Carrera Panamericana.

D-type Jaguar, Le Mans, 1957.

a lesser but still nasty accident in the 1957 Mille Miglia, when the Ferrari driven by the Marquis de Portago crashed into the crowd killing the driver, his navigator and eleven others. It was the end of the Mille Miglia, for over such a route it was impossible to guarantee policing everywhere. Most other races were held on closed circuits, and at these new measures were taken to ensure the safety of the crowds. Hitherto it had been generally accepted that motor racing was dangerous: protection for the onlookers ranged from a row of straw bales to a polite request that the spectators stand back a bit. No longer would this suffice: earth banks were erected, railings circumscribed the course, roads were widened, wire netting was put up and trees were felled. Gradually order was restored and racing recommenced, but for the rest of 1955 it took place under a shadow, and at the end of the season Mercedes-Benz withdrew from racing.

Their objects were not entirely achieved, for the planned development of their GP car involved the progressive increase of its engine power from 250 bhp at the beginning of 1954 to 400 in 1957, when it was anticipated that all four wheels of the car should be driven. A number of other firms withdrew their support from racing in the aftermath of the Le Mans disaster, but the withdrawal of Lancia was due to the firm's commercial difficulties. Unable to sustain the expenditure necessary to keep their cars competitive, Lancia disposed of cars, spares, and designer Jano, to Ferrari, whose own machines had failed miserably in the face of much more modern designs from his rivals. In Ferrari's hands the Lancia was greatly modified, and not always for the better, but it was good enough to carry Fangio to his fourth world championship in 1956. He was to win his fifth, driving a Maserati, in 1957; but beneath him the old order was changing, and there were newcomers ready to take the places yielded by the departed.

It was hardly surprising that this want should be supplied by the British; it was only surprising that it had taken them so long. Their manufacturers had continued weak and ineffectual, in complete contrast to the health of the sport in Britain where its popularity had soared with incredible rapidity in the past years. Because the nation's major motor manufacturers were either indifferent or inept, the countless budding backyard specialists had to blossom in the light of other enterprises, whose sponsorship was frequently so commercially-minded that they were unlikely to be checked in their career by the wave of moralizing that swept Europe after the Le Mans disaster. Accordingly the British Grand Prix was held in due course, and was won by Mercedes-Benz in due course; but it was interesting for the presence of other cars that gave a taste of things to come. There were a couple of Vanwalls, four Connaughts (one with a beautiful aerodynamic body which proved quite impractical when work had to be done on the car in the pits), and a Cooper driven by a scarcely known Australian named Jack Brabham. The Cooper was particularly

Moss triumphant in the Vanwall at Pescara in 1957, winning the GP by three whole minutes.

intriguing: reverting fondly to the rear-engined configuration that had so naturally suited their motorcycle-engined Formula 3 cars, the firm had built a sports car with an 1100 c.c. engine in its tail and it was this, modified to accept a 2·2-litre Bristol engine but retaining the central seat and all-enveloping body of the original, that Brabham drove in the race. As it happened it was the slowest car there, but it was also the first rear-engined Formula 1 car to be raced in an international event since the passing of the days of Auto-Union; with Brabham as its driver, it accounted for two straws in the wind.

A third, almost unaccountable, lent great significance to the last Grand Prix of the 1955 European season at Syracuse. This Sicilian event was expected to be a walkover for Maserati, but the best of them were outdriven and outpaced by the latest version of the Connaught driven by an intelligent, young, and meticulously precise, driver, C. A. S. Brooks. Without a great deal of experience since he began his racing career as a 20-year old dental student in 1952, without ever having raced abroad, without ever having driven a Formula 1 car before, he won by over fifty seconds after three times breaking the lap record, becoming the first British driver to win a Grand Prix in a British car since the 1924 San Sebastian GP, when Segrave's winning Sunbeam was merely a supercharged version of the 1922 Fiat. This Syracuse victory was also important in that it was the first Grand Prix to be won by a car equipped with disc brakes, the last by a car with a Wilson preselector gearbox.

As far as Connaught were concerned, it was a flash in the pan; but the occasion can be seen as beginning a

Journalist Gregor Grant driving a Lotus 1100 in the 1957 Mille Miglia.

period of more active and competitive participation by British manufacturers, as became evident in 1956 when BRM and Vanwall proved to have uncommonly powerful and fast 4-cylinder cars. The BRM was a lot simpler in concept than its predecessor, but just as unreliable, and gave Tony Brooks a bad time during the season when he had been engaged to drive it. The Vanwall had been completely revized, its original humdrum chassis being replaced by a proper spaceframe designed by young Colin Chapman, whose extraordinary success with a series of home-built Lotus sports cars had recommended him as a consultant to the bearing manufacturer Anthony Vandervell who was the driving spirit behind the Vanwall. Together with an exceptionally efficient streamlined body designed by the aerodynamicist Frank Costin, and with an engine that was an amalgam of Norton, Rolls-Royce, and Bosch experience, the Vanwall began to be suddenly competitive, especially on high-speed circuits where it sometimes proved to be the fastest car of all in a straight line. In 1957 the Vanwall was the fastest car in racing; but it suffered an infuriating series of minor troubles which prevented the team drivers Stirling Moss and Tony Brooks from amassing more than three victories between them. As for the V8 Ferrari, now scarcely recognizable as the original Lancia from which it was developed, it could seldom offer a serious challenge, in particular suffering repeated tyre troubles: Ferrari had made an unwise contractual engagement with Englebert some years earlier and was suffering more and more each year thereby. The Maserati, was developed in 1956 when Moss was driving it, and now it was being driven by Fangio as though the man were possessed of demons.

Perhaps he was. Certainly there was something special about this Italian-blooded Argentinian, a man old enough to be father of most of the drivers who sought vainly to compete with him. Born in 1911, he had begun racing in 1934, making himself a great reputation in the phenomenal long-distance road-races of South America in a succession of Fords and Chevrolets. After a brief visit to Europe in 1948 he drove there for a full season in the following year in a Maserati, winning half a dozen Grands Prix and a contract to drive for Alfa Romeo. The highlights of his subsequent career have been touched on in previous pages, but his performance in the 1953 Mille Miglia deserves special mention: although the steering of his Alfa Romeo had come adrift during the race so that only one front wheel answered the helm, he finished second. The man was amazing: apparently immune to fatigue, heat, rain, or cold, he often appeared a forceful driver but seldom broke his car. As for his cornering skills, they seemed quite uncanny, and he was never really outdriven in a Grand Prix car.

It was in the German GP of 1957, in his last full season before retirement, that he gave the most frightening demonstration of his courage and talent. Realizing in practice how strong was the opposition likely to be offered by Hawthorn and Collins in Ferraris, he chose to start with his fuel tanks half-empty. This would enable him to enjoy a lighter and therefore faster and better-handling car, and by making a sprint start he might also enjoy an empty road ahead of him; on the other hand was the fact that he would be forced to make a pit stop for refuelling when his rivals might easily run the entire race non-stop. The severity of his self-imposed task was revealed on the very first lap when, despite having all tanks full, Hawthorn put in a first lap almost equal to the existing lap record, and set a new one on the next lap. For his part, Fangio raised the record even further on the third lap and proceeded to go faster and faster, so that, despite an almost traitorously lethargic fifty-six seconds needed by his mechanics to refuel the Maserati and change its tyres, Fangio was able to recapture the lead he lost during that interval and, by continuing to break the record on every succeeding lap, using all his car's abilities, all the road, and sometimes a measure of the grass, he won by a margin that was adequate even if it could never have been described as comfortable. He was, and his pride insisted on his being, the greatest Grand Prix driver in the world; and there were tears in his eyes when he came back to the pits at Monza after practising for the 1957 Italian GP. For the first time in years he had been unable to secure pole position on the grid, having been beaten in practice by the Vanwalls. The four cars on the front row of the starting grid gave the intensely patriotic Italian crowd a shock: the three in pride of place were green, only Fangio's lightweight 6-cylinder Maserati contributing a touch of Italian racing red to the first rank. The old order was changing visibly.

It was scheduled to change even more. The formula that had prevailed since 1954 was due to expire at the end of 1957. However, when the time came to evolve a new one there was little or no enthusiasm for any significant change, for race promoters, drivers and car manufacturers alike had found that racing had been as fast, as dramatic, and at least as profitable, as at any time in the past. Only the oil companies were unhappy with the regulations as they stood, preferring for commercial reasons that all fuels other than petrol should be forbidden; they could then advertize a victory as having been won on fuel such as the public could buy from ordinary filling stations. Already the financial support of the oil companies was of considerable importance if the Grand Prix world were to continue living in the style to which it had been accustomed, and these views had to be respected.

The only other objection of note to the continuation of the existing formula was that many race promoters wanted races to be shorter. Motor racing was becoming more and more a kind of entertainment, rather than a serious sport, let alone a proving ground for advanced technology; the promoters, recognizing this trend and wanting to put on variety shows rather than simple classical Grands Prix that

In the 1957 Mille Miglia, at the same spot as Grant's Lotus pictured on page 173, veteran Italian racing motorcyclist and driver Piero Taruffi goes through in the 4-litre Tipo 335 Ferrari. Despite his distinguished record, victory in the Mille Miglia had remained his ambition; in this, his fourteenth attempt and the last time the race would be held, Taruffii was successful. It was the crash of a similar Ferrari driven by the Marquis de Portago which brought the history of the Mille Miglia to an end; it was victory which enabled Taruffi then to retire from racing.

lasted for the greater part of a day, argued that if races were made shorter, other races could be held on the same day to build up a supporting programme that would do wonders for the box-office.

These two demands combined to interesting effect. The cars should be slower on petrol, but with their more modest fuel consumption and the reduction in length of the race, their fuel loads would be only half of what they had been in the full-length races of the era ending in 1957, so the cars would actually be quicker. The change in fuels brought greater problems to some manufacturers than to others: the Vanwall for example suffered a loss of about 30 bhp during the winter, but refinements to the rest of the car allowed it to emerge as the most successful of the 1958 season. Moss and Brooks won half a dozen Grands Prix between them, and the Vanwall won the manufacturers' championship, but what was important was that no car remotely resembling it would ever win that again.

All sorts of changes were taking place, and the appearance in 1958 of some lightweight rear-engined Coopers emphasized the doubts that were spreading about how best to design a racing car, how best to reconcile the dictates of experience and the promptings of logic. The end of 1957 may accordingly be seen as the end of the traditional front-engined alcohol-burning understeering long-distance Grand Prix road racing car. If the Vanwall survived successful for another season, it was only as the last representative of outmoded practice which, as we saw in 1934, often staves off the challenge of new technologies. It was indeed the apotheosis of the vintage car; and even in 1958 it had in sundry ways been devalued compared with 1957.

The whole face of racing was changing correspondingly: the Mille Miglia was finished, alcohol fuels were finished, the supercharger had long gone, races were to be much shorter, circuits more artificial – and most of the leading participants in top-class racing would have to get their tyres elsewhere, for after buying them from Pirelli for all those decades, they would be able to do so no longer. The Italian firm, whose products had supported the victorious cars in countless first-class races, with only the German teams and the British sports cars, and occasionally Ferrari, taking their custom elsewhere, took this year of change as occasion to withdraw from racing so as to concentrate on the development of their new radial-ply road tyre, the Cinturato.

Even the Targa Florio was different: after all those years of Italian domination from 1930, punctuated only by Frazer-Nash in 1951 and by Mercedes-Benz in 1955, the race had been won by a Porsche in 1956 and, from 1958, would be consistently fought only by Porsche. Indeed, the only place where the major events continued unchanged after 1957 was America – and her turn would come before long.

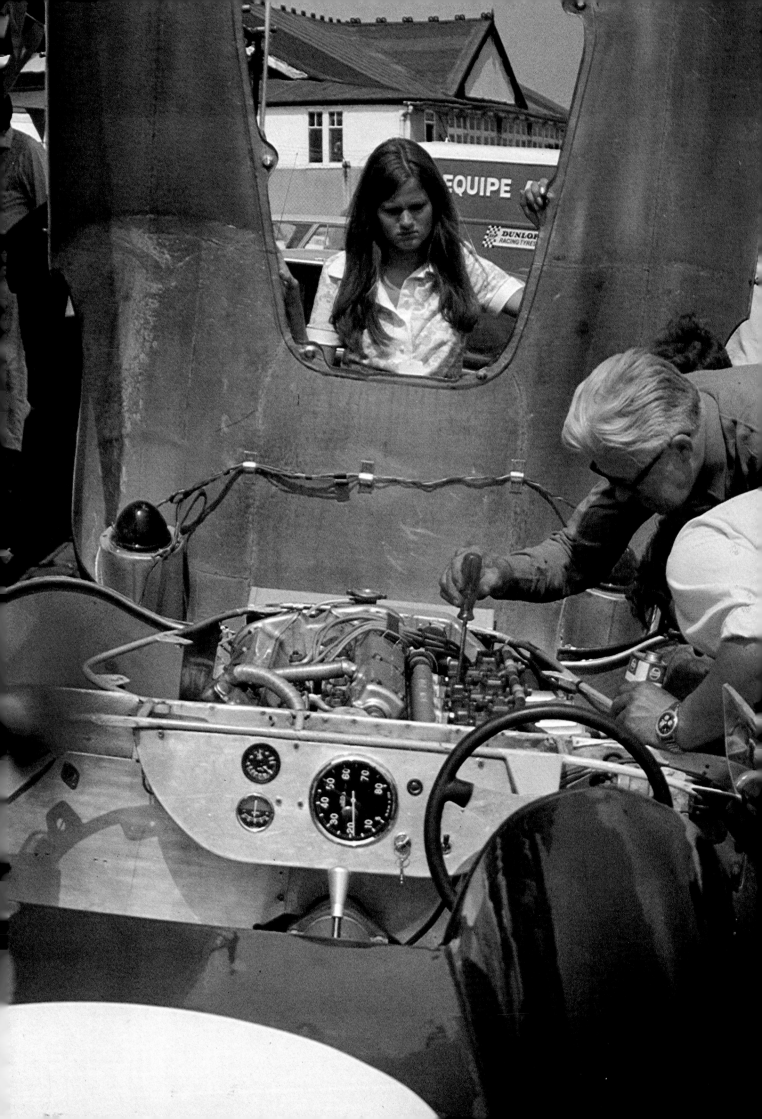

CHAPTER FOUR

THE TOBACCO-FLAVOURED, CANDY-COLOURED, RUBBER-FEATURED SLIDE SHOW
1958–1969

These were the years when everything went back into the melting pot. The sport became popular, and therefore commercial, and therefore tumultuously competitive. Chassis disappeared (so did drivers!), tyres grew squat, wings sprouted, and only in rallying did the engine sometimes stay in front of the driver. Minor events proliferated, saloon car races and club activities, drag festivals and droll kartings, while Indianapolis, like all of America, was transformed.

All of a sudden it seems, only nobody notices the time it takes from back, going back a bit to Jack Brabham with a Bristol engine behind him and the whole of a Gee Pee field in front of him, Silverstone all around him, back in the days when Tony Brooks still wasn't the first British driver to ::::: all of a sudden the whole thing is turned about face and nothing is the same any more, the cars, the drivers, the priorities, the whole thing from the box-office monitor to the RAC Steward and Clerk of the Course, all turned round and facing the other way because all of a sudden we have discovered what makes sense. Benz sense. John Cooper has built a car on a shoestring with a gas torch and put the driver before the engine, the cart before the horse, hysteron proteron, and this oppressively quiet blue-chinned Australian Jack Brabham with his chin down and his head tucked sideways into the corners and a chuckle getting lost somewhere before, before, nobody can keep up with him to hear it, only The Last of the Gentleman Entrants having given up driving a great Delahaye to the greater glory of Goodwood has had Rob Walker Racing Blue painted over another Cooper and Stirling Moss, God's Gift to Jewish motor racing and the First of the Great Professionals (only isn't that what they said about Segrave or was it Guinness, Kenelm Guinness or Algy Guinness, if not Dick Seaman?), is driving it and that takes some staying in front of. Everything else is behind, where the engine should be. The whole thing is turned around, not just the car, the whole picture, with the tacks on the

Many drivers loathed the Spa-Francorchamps circuit, extremely fast and evidently frightening. Freak rainstorms could make it even worse, as in the 1966 Belgian GP when cars left the road in all directions.

frame showing and the painted canvas to the wall, and it's not a bit of good everybody backtracking on what they used to say about the Auto-Union because that was not the beginning nor the end of it. Even the Benz sense has to go back a bit to Doktor Rumpler and his teardrop saloon of 1914 that everybody thought weird who thought.

Weeirrd, that was it in an everted nutwall shell. There was this Benz at Monza in 1924, the Tropfwagen, the teardrop car, and it was the good Doktor Rumpler again, the Man Who Drew Tears – especially because he and the folks at Benz didn't know, weren't to know, about Fiat and their superchargers. The Benz engine, well it was an engine, you know? a nice engine, sort of a very slightly earlier Fiat engine only nobody noticed anything about it except that it was in back of the driver in an aluminium egg of a car, and it went nicely and quite fast but at Monza with the Fiats wailing howl-oowwll-ooowwwlll-ooowwwwllll through four super charging gears who was going to be impressed if the Benz driver got there before his engine did?

It made a pretty two-seater, though, and Adolf Rosenberger who had worked with the Good Doktor at the tear-well got one and drove it in hillclimbs and sports-car races and did well. A good driver, he was, and no less a Meister than Rudi the great Caracciola to measure the proof. Put them both in big 6-cylinder Mercs and there would be no telling, Caratsch beating Rosenberger at the Ring, round the roundy reeling Ring of the Niebelungen in 1927 and Rosenberger outhilling him uprun at Freiburg the same year. Only Caracciola was a professional and Rosenberger a wealthy amateur. So why does Adolf have to go and join up with an electricity-crazy son-of-a-tinsmith Ferdinand ex-Austro-Daimler ex-Daimler-Benz Porsche in 1930 in a Stuttgart design consultancy? Whyever, but Porsche has ideas for a rear-engined racer for somebody, anybody, to make for 1934 and Rosenberger knows enough about rear-engined cars to tell Porsche more than he wants to understand. And when Auto-Union say Let's have it and Porsche says I've got it he doesn't tell them unduly about Rosenberger's part in the P-Wagen, Rosenberger is not there, Adolf Rosenberger has ceased to exist, Adolf the Gifted Amateur Rosenberger was a Jew which is a Great thing to be, the greatest, only not there and then because Hitler was coming to power and then and there Adolf Erstwhile Rosenberger got out of it in the nick of time and went to America and an assumed name. Nobody was going to tell the world that fifty percent of the Great Nazi Motor Racing Blitzkrieg, half of the Kraft durch Freude, was anything to do with a Jew. Least of all Porsche, who did not even advertize the fact that all the detail of the Peawagon Auto Union was done by his assistant Karl Rabe, Dr. Ing. F. Porsche merely giving him the broad general outlines, already smudged because Porsche understood suspension about the same as Hitler understood Jews. This was why the V16 Auto-Unions didn't handle, nothing to do with rear engines, and this was why nobody made much of the fact that Eberan von Eberhorst designed the 3-litre V12 Auto-Unions, and there was nothing much wrong with them except that they would have been better made by Mercedes-Benz.

It should have been Merc who made the rear-engined car, Auto-Union who kept the motor in front. Porsche had always

been a front-engine man; he had started out as a front-wheel-drive man, and you can't get more out front than that. In Daimler-Benz they had Wagner, who had been directly concerned with the 1924 Teardrop in the days when Benz were just that; and they had Doktor Hans Niebel as technical director, and he had been with Benz before the amalgamation too, and the whole three-pointed star in the Ring of the Niebel ought to have been orchestrated by Wagner into a rear-engined Rumpler of the motoring bedsheets, the Twilight of the Gods of motor racing twenty-five freaking years before at long tubewelding last John Cooper of Surbiton Surrey put the power of a Coventry Climax behind Jack Brabham and Stirling Moss and Bruce McLaren and the fear of God into all Italy. Weird, everybody said, and all their Wimbledon necks went SNAP between collar and dropping chins as the Coopers whizzed zizzed past on their quiet powerdown way : : : : : way ahead of all the powerhigh Ferraris and Tec-Mecs and musty fusty gusticars that belonged to way back whenever, sunt lacrimae rerum, the Gilted Amateur and the whole highcollar backdrop of rising-front Europe and the Great American Hangfire. Wee, weeiirrd and the little low Coopers barrel through the corners while the Fazzazz-merchants roll everything from their eyes downwards and if only they had time to look back and see the future, overtaking them, lapping them again, running away on their little tyres and hiding in their diminutive distance and lapping them in great swathes of noisy windingsheets all ready for burial . . .

Back-to-front! Of course . . .

Clark's 2-litre Lotus 33 in the pits before the 1966 Monaco GP, sporting the new low-profile tyres. Above, the small saloons class lined up at Zandvoort in the Tulip Rally, just a few years earlier, reveal far more variety than racing cars were to display.

Cooper started the revolt, and Lotus turned it into a revolution. It wanted no more than the evidence of these two manufacturers' success to stampede all other participants in their wake, and it took only a couple of years for the whole thing to be over and done with. Whereas in 1958 the rear-engined car was a rarity on the starting grid of a Formula 1 race, in 1961 the front-engined car could be considered extinct. The Cooper might not have much power, but it was so tiny and so light that it had a better ratio of power to weight than anything since the V16 BRM finished its unhappy career in 1953, and a better ratio of power per square foot of frontal area than anything since the $4\frac{1}{2}$-litre V12 Ferrari that was last seen racing in that same year. More to the point, it went round corners faster than any racing car that had ever been seen, and it allowed the drivers to make the most of suspension that was for the first time made adjustable in its geometry as well as its elasticity, so that it could be set up to suit their wishes and a given track's demands. With the wiley Brabham (whose trackcraft was as highly developed as his driving skill) at the wheel, it gathered the manufacturers' and drivers' world championships in 1959 and 1960; but by the end of the latter year, the new Lotus 18 had supplanted it as the fastest car in racing.

Colin Chapman, the Lotus designer, had already built a Formula 1 car, a tiny slim and exquisite projectile that looked like a quintessential Vanwall, and was on paper a very much better car, but which was undeservedly unsuccessful on the track. It had much in common with his far more successful ultra-

Brutally powerful and very non-standard, the 3-litre Austin-Healeys prepared by the British Motor Corporation's competitions department ran riot through the rallies of the early 1960s. The top one is getting attention at Inverary in the 1960 RAC Rally; Timo Makinen is well on the way to Monte Carlo in the other . . . but when he won that classic event, in 1965, he was driving a Mini.

lightweight sports-racing cars, which had done so well in major and minor events, even at Le Mans where it made the similarly small French cars look so pathetic by comparison that the organizers found the flimsiest of pretexts to disqualify it, causing Chapman to swear that he would never go there again. The principles by which he had been guided in designing these cars were no longer valid for Formula 1, however, and in 1959 he started afresh to make a car that would employ with the utmost economy the potentiality of every bit of tyre rubber that it could put on the road. He achieved this in a car that looked superficially crude, a box-like affair no part of which other than the windscreen stood higher than twenty-eight inches above the ground, but which concealed between its slab sides a masterpiece of geometrical refinement, structural efficiency, and mechanical simplicity. At a time when it seemed that the driver now constituted the limit of irreducible frontal area, Chapman required him to lie back in his seat, and thus reduced the frontal area even more; but his most important achievement was in devising a new suspension system that gave the car even more astonishing powers of roadholding and handling than the Cooper displayed. It was the Coopers who accomplished the major revolution by devizing simple and compact rear-engined cars that overthrew the established masters, but it was Chapman who led the new praesidium, and it was the Lotus that all other constructors were to copy in the years ahead.

When the 1960 season opened at Monaco, most of them had got no further than copying Cooper, and the race was won comfortably by Stirling Moss in the new Lotus 18. As usual the race was limited to the fastest 16 cars in practice, and the pace of development was illustrated by the fact that the slowest of these lapped half a second faster than the fastest car of 1959.

Unfortunately the Lotus fortunes were often squandered in poor workmanship or materials, if not in skimped safety margins, and accidents were frequent. One of these, at the Goodwood Easter meeting of 1962, put paid to the competitive career of Stirling Moss. Just a year earlier he had proved himself the greatest driver of his time in two performances of outstanding virtuosity, at Monaco and at the Nürburgring, when he drove the 1½-litre Lotus 18 to its absolute limits to win from far more powerful Ferrari opposition.

A new Formula 1 had come into effect in that year, limiting engines to 1½ litres, forbidding the supercharger, specifying commercial pump petrol as the fuel, and setting 450 kilogrammes as the minimum weight for the car in full running order save for being empty of fuel. The formula was also expressive of the new attention to safety that had sprung up since 1955: dual braking circuits were obligatory, the driver had to be able to get in or out without opening or removing any sort of panel, and had to be protected from the

The Mini was the enfant terrible *of the early 1960s, tearing its tyres across every course in the sporting calendar. By 1967, tyres had assumed an importance, and a shape, that would have seemed strange a decade earlier even to a racing man with such bitter experience of them as Ferrari.*

consequences of capsizing by a safety crash bar which usually took the form of a tubular hoop as high as his head and as wide as his shoulders. The safety of others was considered in requiring cars to be oil-tight – a rule that had been in force at Indianapolis for many years and was overdue in Europe. Finally the engine had to be equipped with its own starter and had to rely upon it: the days of the crank-handle or the run-and-bump were over.

It was all very interesting, but the British manufacturers were bitterly opposed to it, and spent some time in vain protests. Lotus, Cooper, and their lesser compatriot copyists, all were chassis manufacturers, content to buy their engines from Coventry Climax or anybody else, only BRM being competent to make their own and even then not very quick about it. Accordingly the British constructors preferred to rely upon their chassis designs to see them through, leaving it to the Germans and Italians to make powerful new engines. It seemed that they would never learn that it takes longer to copy an engine than it does to copy a chassis, but the lesson was repeated to them in 1961 when Ferrari fielded some rear-engined cars with new V6 engines that were considerably more powerful than anything the British could offer, in chassis that might be inferior but were still good enough to allow the cars to match the performance of anything not being driven by Stirling Moss. For a little while, the new domination of Grand Prix racing by British cars and drivers was interrupted: A Ferrari won the 1961 championship, but the greatest surprise to traditionalists was that the car was driven by an American, Phil Hill.

The wave of enthusiasm for motor sport that had swamped Europe in the 1950s had also swept across the United States, which could now muster a respectable number of first-class drivers. Perhaps more to the point, this incredible popularity of the sport had made it more populous, more busy, more avidly pursued by a greater number of more varied people, than ever in its history; and the variety of forms that it took was rivalled only by the multiplicity of venues where it took place.

Even something so apparently irrelevant as the introduction in 1959 of the Mini by what was then the British Motor Corporation had its repercussions: such was the agility and stability of this remarkable little economy saloon that countless young enthusiasts turned to it as a vehicle for sublimating their thwarted desires to go motor racing, tuning it and modifying it and finally learning with any luck to master its idiosyncracies of handling. It made a tremendous impact on the sport, but nowhere greater than in the Monte Carlo Rally.

The regulations for this event had been modified for 1961 to reduce the advantage of big powerful cars on the special stages and hill climbs that were so important in determining the results, the original idea being a French one because at the time the French had some small cars (such as the Panhard) which could profitably exploit the new rules. For that one year the plan succeeded, but in 1962 and 1963 the French were thwarted by the Swede Erik Carlsson in an 850 c.c. Saab. By this time, BMC had formed an alliance with Cooper which resulted in a high-performance Mini-Cooper that was admirably suited to rally work on winter roads, and in 1964 the rally was won by the Irishman Paddy Hopkirk.

He became famous as the arch exponent of a new style of driving, one to which the front-wheel-drive Mini was supremely well adapted: it relied on free use of the handbrake to set the tail of the car sliding in whatever direction the driver chose, the Mini adopting some incredible attitudes on the way into and through a tight slippery-surfaced corner as, with the power sustained throughout, the front wheels did the driving and the rear wheels did the steering. The principle was one that had been evolved in Ireland, where a popular form of sport was the driving-test meeting, a delightfully informal affair that was conducted at any convenient country crossroads where cars would be flicked and twitched forwards backwards and sideways at high speed into a carefully choreographed sequence of 'Parking' manoeuvres, danced against a stopwatch. Developing these techniques, Hopkirk showed that it was possible to flick the Mini through 180 degrees and continue in the original direction in reverse gear, and then to repeat the flick so as to resume

A Mini was not essential in autocross mud, but lots of people found it more fun that way.

forward travel, still in the same direction; or alternatively the whole sequence could be smoothed into a 360-degree flick spin during which the car would continue along a road which might not be much wider than the length of the car. Given such virtuosity, merely to get around a corner seemed child's play, and Hopkirk's display in the snowbound Alps was the talking point of the year. However, with rallying becoming more and more a winter business of loose or slippery surfaces and less and less like a politely quiet kind of road racing with the emphasis on navigation, so the appropriately specialized skills of Scandinavian drivers brought them to the fore. Some of them learned to keep both hands on the steering wheel, ignoring the handbrake and instead kicking at the brake pedal with the left foot while keeping the engine on the boil with the right, doing any necessary gear-changing without reference to the clutch pedal. One of the very fastest of these virtuosi was a Finn, Timo Mäkinen, who was at that time also a member of the BMC rally team, and in 1965, when the Monte Carlo rally was nearly wiped out by a blizzard, he won it in a Mini-Cooper after a drive that deserves to be remembered as one of the most phenomenal in history. He should have won again in 1966, but the French – than whom of course none could be more Chauvinistic – sought to have the car disqualified because they alleged that its quartz-iodine lamp bulbs infringed the regulations. This led to a tremendous dispute, and a good deal of Anglo-French vituperation, the outcome of which was that the predominantly French tribunal upheld the objection, so that victory could be attributed to a Citroën. After that, nobody was going to let such a peculiar set of rules prevail any longer, and the rally

The Lotus Cortina, Mark 1, was meant to be taken seriously, even in the 1966 RAC Rally.

became a scratch event in time for another Finn, Rauno Aaltonen, to score another Mini-Cooper win in 1967. That was practically the end of the Mini-Cooper's international competition career, and for the next three years Porsche reigned over Monte Carlo until the curvaceous little Alpine-Renault toppled them.

Meanwhile the Mini-Cooper had been going great guns on the racing circuits, where events for saloon cars, more or less modified according to various sets of rules that became bewildering in their variety, acquired tremendous popularity among drivers and spectators alike. For a while, Jaguar saloons had been the fastest on the tracks of Britain and Germany, but often the Mini-Cooper was cast in the role of giant-slayer, especially when weather conditions were bad and the little car could be powered sideways through all its corners without burning too much of its tyres away in clouds of rubber smoke. Nothing was faster into a corner than a well-set-up Mini; but the small Ford saloons, whose engines were amenable to much more tuning, were frequently faster out of it, and saloon-car racing became a furious barging match from start to finish. By 1965, however, brute force was beginning to prevail on the circuits of Britain, and many of the major saloon car races were won by large American cars (notably the Ford Galaxie, Fairmont and Mustang) which enjoyed far more power than anything else and were able to exploit the new ultra-wide racing tyres that were coming into circulation from the American manufacturers Firestone and Goodyear. There was only one car of modest size that could rival and often defeat these monsters, and that was the Ford Lotus Cortina – especially when driven by Jim Clark.

*In track racing, the Lotus Cortina had to be taken
seriously; in 1963 it was already one of the fastest saloons
around Brands Hatch. And of course Daimler-Benz
continued to take everything seriously, including dusty open-
road events in Argentina where success strengthened their
healthy position in the South American market.*

This shy, quiet, nail-biting young Scot was one of the two or three most superb drivers the world ever saw, perhaps the most gifted of them all. He was a natural genius, able to extract the utmost from any kind of cars, anxious to try anything and everything on wheels. Encouraged by friends he began racing regularly in 1958 at the age of 22, against some parental opposition, faring so well that several sports-car teams sought his services. By 1960 he had settled into the Lotus team, forming a remarkably close working relationship with Chapman. He needed only a little experience to bring out his abilities as a Grand Prix driver, and by 1961 he was as fast as Moss. With Jimmy's help, Chapman was making rapid progress in the development of the racing Lotus, and in 1962 he brought out the monocoque Lotus 25, a slim and beautiful little projectile which, like other Loti before it, became the model for all other manufacturers to copy so that within very few years the simple multi-tubular racing car chassis had become a thing of the past. In the Lotus 25 Clark won his first really important race, the Belgian GP, and would have been world champion for 1962 had not his Climax engine failed in the last race, leaving the title to Graham Hill in the more powerful BRM. In 1963 he won ten Grands Prix and was a deserving champion, as again in 1965; but even in those years when circumstances prevented him from winning the title, nobody was in any doubt that Jimmy was the supreme driver of his day.

Perhaps the last to be convinced were the Americans, but when he went to Indianapolis in 1963 with a Lotus built around a Ford V8 for that event, they were overwhelmed by his ability. The car they viewed with derision, funny little rear-engined toy that it looked among the hulking great front-engined beam-axled blasters that were the traditional weapons for this frightful affray; but in it Clark was so much faster than everything else that they were shaken rigid, and the tyre troubles that forced him down to second place saved them from considerable embarrassment – not to mention giving them time to start copying the Lotus, just as all Europe's racing car manufacturers had done. Yet it was Clark's competence that impressed them just as much as the car's: the Indianapolis regulars had always treated a spin as something terminal – if the car started to spin, well, brother, that was it, we don't call it a spin-out for nothing – but then Clark got into a spin, controlled it through a full gyration and continued non-stop. The crowd was amazed; when he did it again, they were abashed. The Lotus was not the only setter of new standards in America that day. His car failed there in 1964, but when it won in 1965 he had lifted the average speed of the race to 150 mph from the 140 at which it stood when he first visited the track.

The performance of Clark and the Lotus was all that was needed to complete the emancipation of motor sport in the USA. For some years it had been growing increasingly rich in variety. Road-racing events

Americans just love accelerating: they go drag-racing on sand . . .

attracted amateur clubmen whose tastes ran to European sports cars; hundreds of little oval tracks, often shorter than half a mile and often dirt-surfaced, accommodated frantic weekly meetings of modified stock cars and midget single-seaters; thirty odd steeply banked oval super-speedways (many in the south-eastern States) echoed to the thunder of highly-tuned 'stock' cars, ostensibly production saloons but extensively and expensively modified to meet the rules of NASCAR (the National Association for Stock Car Auto Racing), slip-streaming at speeds up to 200 mph and driven by tough middle-aged men whose traditions went back to 'moonlighting', the illicit rum-running in which many of the leading racing men developed their driving skills during the prohibition era. Then there were the drag strips, more than 160 of them, attracting six million Americans each year to marvel at frantically powerful special-purpose cars sprinting in pairs over an electronically timed quarter of a mile: by 1967 the seven seconds mark had been beaten, Don Prudhomme recording an elapsed time of 6·92 seconds for the standing-start quarter-mile in a Chrysler-engined dragster at Carlsbad, California.

All these affairs were as noisy, colourful and spectacular as only the Americans know how to make them or indeed to enjoy them. Most of them reflected a traditional American approach to the idea of motor sport, in which speed was at a premium and cornering at a discount. The ultimate expression of all this was the annual gathering on the Bonneville Salt Flats in Utah, the scene since 1935 of all attempts to raise the world land speed record which a series of jet-engined devices lifted rapidly from the 403 mph of the late

... and on tarmac strips, chemically treated to improve traction at the start of the measured quarter mile.

Donald Campbell's Bluebird in 1964 to the 600·6 mph of Craig Breedlove's Spirit of America in 1965.

By 1966, America had a new and fascinating class of racing to explore, a series of sports-car races shared with the Canadian Automobile Sports Clubs and known as the CanAm (Canadian-American) series. The races were professional affairs staged on half a dozen assorted but generally short and sinuous road-racing circuits in the two countries, and the cars were what were then known as Group 7 sports-racing two-seaters. In effect they combined the chassis and suspension technologies of the European Grand Prix car with very highly tuned large-capacity engines based on American stock block production V8s, housed in stylishly (if not always very efficiently) streamlined open two-seater bodies bereft of lights or any of the other refinements by which a sports car may be recognized as something more than a mere racer. These cars were prodigiously fast and most of the successful ones were of British origin, Lola and McLaren in turn supplying nearly all the winning cars although of course neither could take any credit for the power units. Nevertheless the most significant contribution to the series was made by an American firm, Chaparral, ostensibly headed by a couple of wealthy Texans named Hap Sharp and Jim Hall. In fact the organization was a front for General Motors, who publicly maintained their isolation from motor sport while privily indulging in it by whatever means might be available, thus reaping all possible benefits without risking any loss of reputation if things went wrong.

This does not detract from the tremendous flair displayed by Jim Hall, in particular, as designer and

In the latter 1960s Ferrari, Ford and General Motors fought hard for supremacy in long-distance sports-car races. The P4 Ferrari and the winged 2F Chaparral are at Brands Hatch, the Ford GT40 above at Spa.

driver. He had gone to Europe a few years earlier and bought himself a place in a Lotus from which he could study Grand Prix racing at first hand. By 1963 he was back in America building a rear-engined sports car of very advanced design, and in succeeding years the series 2 Chaparral was given more and more advanced and unorthodox features. A torque-converter transmission was one of the first, followed by a series of aerodynamic refinements: the spoiler at the lip of the tail was not new (it first appeared on a Ferrari in 1961 at the instigation of another American driver, Ritchie Ginther) but the Chaparral was probably the pioneer at this time of spoilers at or beneath the nose of the car, something so effective that they have since spread to even the most mundane of family saloons.

The most significant thing was yet to come. Hall had always worked very closely with Firestone (his Chaparral 2D, a closed car raced in European long-distance sports-car events, had earlier in 1966 been the first to use wide-grooved hand-cut rain tyres to win the 1000-kilometre race at the Nürburgring), and he knew that the latest tyres generated higher cornering forces if subjected to greater downforce than was applied by the weight of the car. An inverted wing or airfoil could develop an aerodynamically induced downforce with the least penalty in weight or drag: the idea had been tried in the past, by Michel May on a Porsche in 1955 and by Opel on a rocket-powered experimental car in the 1920s, but the first thorough development of the idea was by Hall, and its first successful application was the Chaparral 2E which appeared in September 1966 at Bridgehampton. How advanced Hall's thinking was is well illustrated by the fact that the idea was not effectively copied until two years later in Formula 1 Grand Prix racing.

It must be admitted that the Grand Prix establishment had other preoccupations. A new formula had

Jim Clark and Cosworth-Ford engine in the original Lotus 49.

come into effect at the beginning of 1966, a formula expected to restore to Grand Prix racing some of the drama that had been rather missing since the close of the 1960 season. The important change in the rules was an increase in the permitted engine displacement to 3 litres for unsupercharged designs, while the supercharger was once again given its chance with engines of $1\frac{1}{2}$ litres. Retention of the existing fuel regulations made it highly improbable that anybody would build a supercharged car, and most of the other rules were retained as well – including the 1961 ban on bodywork enclosing the wheels, which with ever-growing tyre widths were becoming the major obstacle to aerodynamic cleanliness.

As usual at the beginning of any new formula, there was a lot of confusion about the direction that developments should follow, and very few teams fielded effective new engines in 1966. Ferrari adapted a sports-car V12, Cooper accepted an enlarged Maserati V12, and BRM made a thoroughly disgraceful mess of what could have been an excellent H16. Nearly everybody else made do with what they could get, usually something of 2 or $2\frac{1}{2}$ litres, but Brabham, who had become a manufacturer in his own right in 1962, turned up for the South African GP at East London on New Year's Day 1966 with a new car powered by a 3-litre V8 engine that had been very cleverly based on a production $3\frac{1}{2}$-litre Buick. It was not a very powerful engine, but it was a very flexible and economical one, the whole car was very light and well behaved, and with Brabham driving more smoothly and stylishly than ever before against rivals who appeared more inept than ever before, it carried its maker to the championship that he had last enjoyed in 1960.

Others dreamed of better engines: the Howmet above and the Lotus beneath were both powered by gas turbine.

V12 BRM on the starting line at Silverstone, 1971.

Only towards the end of the year did new purpose-built engines appear. One, an elegant if unreliable V12, powered a car that was driven by the American Dan Gurney, and it was known as the All-American Eagle despite the fact that it was entirely designed and manufactured in England. The other was also a V12, but one of quite exceptional merit and unusual layout. This was the Honda, its engine designed by Shoichiro Irimajiri, a brilliant young man who had made the 1½-litre V12 Honda of 1965 the fastest of its class, and who had earlier been responsible for the best of Honda's all-conquering motorcycle racing engines. This 3-litre Honda was by a comfortable margin the most powerful engine of its time, but it was hampered by a dreadfully heavy chassis. Neither car prospered, and for most of 1967 the two cars of the Brabham team continued to have their own way. Only when the travelling circus arrived at Zandvoort for the Dutch GP did a really effective new car appear, and then Jimmy Clark drove it to victory at its first outing. Ford had come to the aid of Lotus.

Ford of America had been campaigning on a grand scale in European motor racing for some time, spending millions in several fruitless attempts to win the Le Mans 24-hour race with their squat rear-engined GT 40 before a 7-litre Mk. 2 version of it succeeded in 1966. They were to win the race four times in a row, but in the meantime felt able to divert £100,000 to Cosworth Engineering of Northampton (a venture involving Mike Costin and Keith Duckworth) for the preparation of a 3-litre GP engine to be made available initially to Lotus and after a year to all comers. Cosworth built a light and tolerably simple V8 that Chapman treated as a structural member in his new Lotus 49, which immediately assumed first rank in the Formula 1 hierarchy. Although it was successful first time out, the Cosworth Ford engine was unreliable initially, which was why Jimmy Clark failed by a small margin to secure the 1967 title. Very soon, however, it and the Lotus matured into an almost unbeatable combination; but alas, Clark was not long able to exploit it, for on 7 April 1968, while driving his uncompetitive Lotus 48 in an unimportant Formula 2 race

Flat 12 Ferrari emerging from Station Hairpin at Monte Carlo, 1971.

at Hockenheim in Germany, he unaccountably crashed (it was later deduced that a tyre had pulled away from its rim and lost its pressure) and was killed. There was never such a hush as fell upon the motor racing world that Sunday, as the news gradually and quietly spread around all the other active circuits. What seemed impossible had happened, and left a sense of loss that no other driver's departure ever occasioned. The death of Jimmy Clark was like the assassination of John Kennedy: you would always remember exactly where you were and what you were doing when the news of it reached you. There was something else, too, that was strange: the 1968 season was marred by several fatal accidents – but could it be coincidence that the deaths of Jim Clark, Lodovico Scarfiotti, Jo Schlesser and Mike Spence all occurred on the 7th day of the month?

The tyre failure that is believed to have caused Clark's crash was due to a phenomenon not then understood, being associated only with the new generation of low-profile tubeless racing tyres which had gradually been superseding all others in racing since early 1966. It was to exploit their potential that the wing or airfoil already seen on the Chaparral 2E came to be applied to Formula 1 cars during the 1968 season. Its use spread rapidly, and complications proliferated: there were adjustable wings, variable-incidence wings, wings with dihedral, wings at the back and at the front, some of them attached to the body of the car, some to the suspension. Some did not remain attached, and some very nasty accidents ensued. The whole business threatened to get out of hand, and during practice for the 1969 Monaco GP the fate of wings was sealed; in future only a relatively small one, mounted low down and fixed directly to the sprung mass of the car, would be permitted, along with nasal fins of similarly restricted size.

Quickly clipped though it may have been, the wing arrived just in time to nip four-wheel drive in the bud. Several tentative efforts to make four-wheel drive effective in a Formula 1 car were doomed to failure in 1969, including an interesting gas-turbine-engined Lotus derived from a car with which the firm had

Goodness knows what would have happened to the history of motor racing if Ford had successfully concluded their attempts to do a deal with Ferrari in 1963. Instead, negotiations fell through, and in 1964 Ford began their costly campaign to win at Le Mans. For two years, Ferraris held them at bay, but although the Ferrari P4 with its beautiful new 4-litre V12 engine and revised chassis and body scored notable successes at other venues such as Daytona, it was beaten at Le Mans (left, above). In contrast, the early Ford GT40 was a flop at Le Mans (left, below) but a bigger Mark 2 version made history in 1967 by being the first Ford to win there (two Fords attempted a dead heat), the first car to cover more than 3000 miles in the 24 hours, and the first to average more than 200 km/h.

nearly won the 1968 Indianapolis 500, being robbed of victory there only by the most cruel luck. The other four-wheel drive cars were the Cosworth (never raced), the McLaren and the Matra.

This last was a French make, produced by a firm of high repute in the aerospace industry. They had shown great promise with their sports cars and small-capacity single-seaters in recent years, and at the end of 1967 their first Formula 1 car appeared, promising to offer a serious threat to the Lotus 49. The Matra engine was a beautiful V12 that turned out to be impossibly thirsty and insufficiently powerful. For 1969 the superb Matra chassis was fitted with a Cosworth engine, and in the hands of young Jackie Stewart (who had been rapidly working his way to the top since joining the BRM team in 1965) it dominated the season to give him the first of several world championships. This very shrewd and very skilful young man was quick to make the most of the opportunities his new status gave him: but then, as Sir James Barry once observed, *there are few more impressive sights in the world than a Scotsman on the make.*

Other drivers had been described as professional before him, but never had professionalism been so assiduously cultivated as by John Young Stewart. His driving, very quick and clean and determined, was a model for all others of his day to emulate, but most of them found his example of commercial acumen more attractive to follow. The sport was becoming very mercenary indeed. It was also becoming very dangerous (something against which Stewart campaigned in every possible way) as, under the influence of bigger tyres and better wings, cornering speeds rose rapidly and the severity of accidents increased alarmingly. Just one thing made steady progress, and that was the Cosworth engine, to the delight of Ford and the shame of Matra. The figures told the story adequately: in 1956 when Grand Prix racing was at its grandest and perhaps most glorious, there were nine different makes of cars competing, using altogether eleven different types of engine, albeit of just nine makes. By 1968 there were eight makes of cars with seven different engines; and by mid-1970 there were nine cars and six engines. Continue to 1979 and you would find only four engine makers engaged in Formula 1 racing, with the tally of Cosworth victories running to 125. People were beginning to ask, in emulation of Dorothy Parker,

With this the gist and sum of it
What further good can come of it?

The first March GP car makes its debut at Brands Hatch in 1970, above. All along the pits the picture is the same – broad tyres and blatant machinery.

CHAPTER FIVE

DEVOLUTION
1970–1980

> Grand Prix racing sets hard and crystalline, while sports car racing fuses extravagance and absurdity in trying to follow the same course, with amazing results at places like Le Mans and Daytona, now that the great road-races are no more and everything has to happen on a largely artificial track. Now it is the turn of rallying to wax and grow fat, expanding as a sport that maintains identity with the open road, even though much of it be through forest and savannah. Sometimes it is on ice; always it is on tenterhooks; and increasingly it is on radial-ply tyres, which finally break into racing as well . . .

As a general rule, history should not be written until it is old enough to be seen as history. The recent past is always difficult to see in perspective, its personalities too familiar, its sensations too powerful, its direction too indistinct. *World history*, said Schiller, *is the world court of judgement*; and the same applies to any other kind of history, even that of motor sport. It is too early to sit in judgement when the evidence has not all been properly sifted.

It is also too early to put down as history what still comes up as vivid recollection. Our dismay at the death of Jochen Rindt in a Lotus at Monza, shortly before he was proclaimed world champion at the end of 1970, is still as keen as our delight at the success of Mario Andretti in a Lotus, world champion for 1978; and these two results, so widely separated, prompt the recollection that in the decade four makes accounted for all the championships. Three were won in Lotus cars, three in Ferraris, two in a McLaren and two in a Tyrrell. This suggests an uncommon consistency and continuity in Grand Prix racing, and that would be a fair comment on the retrospective picture. The motor racing season is now so hectic, so long and geographically so wide-ranging, that the manufacturers have very little time for the development of really new and original ideas. After the imposition of strict limitations on aerodynamic aids at the end of the 1960s, the continuing trend since the appearance of the Lotus 72 in 1970 has been to devise bodies capable of generating more and more downforce, grinding the tyres harder and harder into the road so that they can develop more and more cornering power, until by 1979 the cornering limit was imposed at some circuits not by any structural considerations or mechanical constraints in the cars, but by the strength of the drivers' necks in supporting their heavy-helmeted heads against the forces involved. Protagoras is as apposite as ever: man is once again the measure . . .

Sometimes motor-racing man measures his achievements in money. Occasionally he makes his métier a thing of the spirit. Very rarely he does both, as in the case of Niki Lauda who fought to survive what should have been a fatal accident in his Ferrari at the Nürburgring during the year of his first world championship in 1975, to become champion in a Ferrari again in 1977 – having conceded the title by just one point to the McLaren driver James Hunt in 1976, when he judged conditions in the Japanese GP too dangerous for him to continue and was brave enough to risk ridicule when he withdrew.

The racing fortunes of Ferrari have likewise been a matter as much of spirit as of substance. Taken under the wing of Fiat at a time when industrial unrest in Italy made the old giant of early racing a patron of uncertain value, Ferrari persevered doggedly with the flat-12 3-litre that had been introduced in 1970. Throughout the first half of that year it was a disappointment, breaking more crankshafts than records; then with a redesign in the autumn of 1970 it suddenly became the fastest car in Grand Prix racing and won four of the last five championship events of the year. Not the least refreshing thing about this was the relief it afforded to the monotony of races being won by Cosworth-engined kit-cars; but the form book was upset again in 1971, for the Ferrari could not maintain its promise and it was Jackie Stewart who became champion again, driving a car built for him by Tyrrell around a Cosworth engine. Matra had made some attempts to raise the tone of racing by bringing out a new V12 engine of their own, but whilst it undoubtedly did wonders for the sound of racing, it achieved little else. The careers of these two 12-cylinder machines made an interesting contrast. While the Ferrari seemed unable to make the grade in Formula 1, a sports car version of it did so well that Ferrari secured the world sports car championship in 1972, some time before the single-seater began to realize their ambitions for it. In the case of Matra, a steady decline in the fortunes of their Grand Prix car was countervailed by a sudden run of successes with a 2-seater version of it, scoring a hat-trick at Le Mans, winning the Tour de France (imagine touring France in one of those!) and capturing the sports car championship twice running in 1973 and 1974.

It may be difficult to see such machines as sports cars, as the term used to be understood, but understandings have changed with the years. In any case, it would be mean to reject them because of their Formula 1 relationships when, in earlier eras of racing, the idea of a GP car with road-going equipment conjured up a picture of the ideal super-sports car as exemplified by the Alfa Romeo that used to win the Mille Miglia in the 1930s, and for that matter the Mercedes-Benz which won it in 1955. It would be even more mean of spirit to complain in the light of comparison with the far more outrageous Porsche cars that had been dominating sports car events in the immediately preceding years. While mildly modified versions of the Porsche 911 production car served countless drivers in all kinds of more modest competition up to and including the level of regular wins in the Monte Carlo rally, Porsche built sports-racing cars that grew rapidly more rabid from year to year, culminating in the enormously powerful 5-litre flat-12 type 917, a car so powerful and purposeful that it could hardly fail to win anything for which it was entered – though occasionally it did. Porsche did not stop even at that: after years of ruinous one-make domination of the CanAm race series on the American continent by the McLaren team, Porsche practically brought the series

to its knees by producing a turbocharged version of the 917. It was a brilliant piece of engineering, but with more than 1000 bhp at its disposal it hardly seemed a realistic motor car.

The turbocharger that made such excesses feasible has been an object of great enthusiasm ever since. More noteworthy in its employment have been Renault, who made a welcome return to the sport with a series of racing 2-seaters, powered by their own little V6 engine, which finally achieved their ambition of an outright victory at Le Mans. This was in 1978 when youthful Didier Pironi and veteran Jean-Pierre Jaussaud combined to shatter existing records for the race, covering more than 3100 miles to average over 131 mph for the 24 hours at the wheel of a dramatically-painted black and yellow Renault, beautifully prepared and presented, propelled by an engine that was physically the smallest ever to power a Le Mans winner. With this ambition realized, Renault were then able to concentrate better on the development of the turbocharged Formula 1 car that they had unveiled in 1977, and after a year of consistent effort and inconsistent results they finally won the race they most wanted to win, the French Grand Prix, only conceding second place to Ferrari after one of the most ferocious high-speed barging matches never to have ended in catastrophe. And if at the end of the year it was Ferrari who emerged as champion manufacturer, with their No. 1 driver Jody Scheckter enthroned as the first South African ever to be world champion driver, then the nationalistic (and indeed nationalized) Régie Renault could console themselves with the thought that they shared with the victors something in common that was French: the two teams both relied on Michelin radial-ply tyres. The last bastion of the bias-play had been broken down.

Nowhere had the success of the radial-ply tyre, by now accepted as the modern norm for ordinary road cars, been more complete or convincing than in rallying. The sport itself seemed more convincing to many who could no longer identify in the decadent denizens of the artificial race tracks anything bearing a sensible resemblance to the road cars with which they were familiar. Rallying was quite different, being designed and carefully regulated to attract cars that were manifestly similar to, if not identical with, production saloons such as might be seen in any street. It was this reason more than any other that assured rallying of enormous popular support throughout the decade, and encouraged the major car manufacturers to enter teams of very highly tuned and elaborately prepared versions of cars that were put into production on a limited series basis with just this object in view. For a long time the most successful at this were Ford, whose British-built Escort scored innumerable successes in the hands of many shrewdly selected star drivers; but with the solitary interruption by Alpine Renault in 1973, the world rally championship for makes was the preserve of the Pirelli-radial-tyred Italians from 1972 onwards, falling on four occasions to Lancia (by now a subsidiary of Fiat) and for the last three years to Fiat themselves. Not that you would describe the Lancia as a saloon; the rear-enged competition Stratos, with its Ferrari Dino V6 engine churning out even more than the 240 bhp that seemed to be the general rule for top-flight rally cars, seemed more like a 2-seater racing hard top – but in theory one would order one from a Lancia dealer, and in fact a number of Stratoi were delivered to private customers, just to rove that it was a production model.

This was by no means a rare deception, for the sport of rallying has grown to be no less deceitful than sports car racing is dishonest. The rot set in during the early 1960s after the invention by Mr. Jack Hemsley of the special stage – not that he could be blamed for so clever a solution to the intractable problems which faced him as organizer of the Royal Automobile Club Rally, the major British event of the year. The laws of England did not and do not admit high-speed motoring competitions to take place on the public highway, so he plotted a route to be covered by competitors at a strictly regulated speed calculated to avoid offence to the public, visiting a series of forest tracks where they could be let loose for a few minutes of timed flat-out sliding and bumping, one at a time and the devil take the hindmost as the ruts are worn deeper. Gradually all other major rallies adopted the same pattern, except the really large-scale affairs, particularly the East African Safari rally which was tantamount to one long special stage in the ragged edge of the rainy season. Thus the ostensibly tourer-based rally car developed a character as artificial as that of any other successful competition vehicle, for in Britain, Northern Europe, and Scandinavia, virtually all rallies were conducted (so far as the crucial special stages were concerned) off the highway in conditions of primitive savagery that qualified them as quite the nastiest cross-country runs since Dante's Inferno. Only in the areas surrounding the Mediterranean were international rallies run on routes that were preponderantly tarmac; elsewhere it was more a matter of rock-jumping and rut-bashing than of road-running, and cars had to be constructed accordingly. It was all a far cry from the modest-paced road events, usually nocturnal and invariably putting

great emphasis on navigational skill, that were the mainstay of rallying in the 1950s in Europe and which were to remain the rule in the USA even into the 1970s.

Indeed, the whole of motor sport is a far cry from what it used to be. Undoubtedly the greatest difference is that there is so much more of it than at any time in the past. America, Britain, France, Italy and not a few other countries are pock-marked with road-racing tracks, dust bowls, hills, forest tracks, disused airfields and cinder arenas, where something noisy and aggressively competitive may be expected to take place practically every weekend of the year. It is the amateurs who offer the most kaleidoscopic variety in Clubman's events, driving weirdly modified saloons, garishly converted sports cars, or minor-league single-seaters, with every motive ranging from pleasure in machinery to hunger for notoriety. Some of them spend a staggering amount of money – not difficult to do when rebuilding a vintage racer or maintaining a lately-outmoded Formula 1 car – while others go in brash search of sponsorship confident that the world owes them a staggering amount of money.

At the professional level, sponsorship – or rather the advertising that makes sponsorship a commercially tenable proposition – has done more to lower the tone of motor sport in a dozen years than all the iniquities of patriotism had done in a period six times as long. The use of the racing car as a mobile advertisement hoarding had been a bizarre feature of racing in America for many years before finally the international governing body of the sport was pressurised into allowing it elsewhere, even on the flanks of Grand Prix cars. At first, advertising decals were only allowed to be of strictly limited and reasonably inoffensive size; but it was not long before somebody (probably the ingenious Colin Chapman himself) realized that since there was no actual compulsion to field cars in the national racing colours, there would be nothing to stop him entering his Team Lotus racers painted overall in a colour scheme that could be associated with the wares of a wealthy tobacco company. So it was that, discarding the traditional yellow-flashed green that

Then the fastest though not the steadiest driver in the Fiat rally team, Marku Alen drove a Lancia Stratos in the 1978 RAC Rally. In that year, Stratos won 21 rallies – but not this one.

Lotus cars had paraded before the world since the 1950s, the Lotus factory cars appeared in 1968 dressed overall like a cigarette packet. It was not the first time that Lotus were to be widely copied, nor would it be the last; but for all his mechanical pioneering, Chapman was probably never as influential as with this feat of commercial sleight-of-hand. Soon every car of note and every car driven by a driver of note was a multi-coloured broth of visual irrelevance, liveried and annotated to promote the names of anything from tyres and spark plugs to contraceptives and cosmetics. Pits and paddocks became more overcrowded than ever before as advertisers, publicists and hangers-on fought for vantage points where the action was busiest and the glamour thickest. The whole business invited disparagement, but it could be argued that to make motor racing a medium for parading the rivalry between cigarette manufacturers was less vicious than the former practice of parading the rivalry between nations.

A more sinister turn was taken when some of the biggest advertisers took to sponsoring complete events, for this provoked a rivalry such as had not been seen (and then on a much more modest scale) since about 1932. This was an entirely self-interested and bitterly acrimonious struggle for influence and control over motor sporting events at their highest and therefore most lucrative level. Race organizers (who were often circuit owners, now that the true road races were almost all supplanted by events in enclosed arenas) formed one of the factions; the entrants, who organized themselves as an association for Formula 1 car constructors, were another; and the sport's governing body was the third, clinging to such vestiges of its

Ford were the most experienced and successful builders of rally cars in the 1970s, their Mark 1 Escort setting an early standard that for some time only the Mark 2 could follow.

erstwhile power as it could preserve from the grasp of these newly rebellious parties which seemed better funded than motor racing's rebels had ever before been.

This tripartite war caused tremendous confusion, which was eventually resolved when the constructors' association did a deal with the race organizers, offering them a more or less guaranteed, standard, carefully wrapped and packaged, series of races for an agreed calendar and an agreed price. An association of racing drivers attempted to intrude by dictating their own terms to the race organizers, recalcitrant circuit owners being terrorized by threatened boycotts on the grounds that the drivers found safety provisions at the track inadequate. Whether because they were a loosely knit bunch of individualists who could not agree among themselves, or because too many of them had sold themselves body and soul to the advertisers whose liveries they wore and whose orders they subsequently had to take, the drivers failed to be an effective force. In the end the struggle for power became a straight fight between two bodies, the car makers and the law makers.

If it was not always clear what the latter wanted, it was always clear what the former did not want. The constructors were not exactly opposed to progress, but rather to change. So long as most of them were small specialist firms using proprietary engines, usually the V8 Cosworth Ford, they rejected any suggestion of a new formula that might require them to cast about for new sources of supply. Hope for salvation came with the return to the sport of some of the great car manufacturers – Renault, Fiat (who had

There is motor sport east of the Iron Curtain, which sometimes parts to let a few competitors through. This Polonez ran in the 1980 Manx Rally.

taken over Ferrari but left the name intact and allowed Ferrari himself to retain control of the racing programme) and Alfa Romeo. It was difficult to imagine the mighty state-owned Règie Renault suffering the glory of France and the prowess of Billancourt to be impeded by some little half-pint assembler of kit cars taking an entrepeneurial stand. However, it was to transpire that the industrial giants had no monopoly of brains.

It costs a great deal of money to make a modern racing car. To find it suddenly rendered obsolete by some new and revolutionary principle of design can cause acute inflammation of the budget, if not chronic impairment of the zeal; and if a manufacturer be so high and so mighty as to be able to survive the financial loss, he is thereby less likely to be able to survive the embarrassment.

All this was revealed in the pitiless light of the 1980 Grand Prix season, during the course of which the fastest car at any circuit was usually either a Renault or a Williams. On circuits where there were sufficient lengths of reasonably straight road, the Renault could use the superior performance of its turbocharged engine to pull away from all its rivals; on circuits where this advantage could not be exploited, the Williams made the most of superior aerodynamics and related chassis design to outperform everything else. Since the English car enjoyed better reliability, probably better driving, and possibly better luck, the year closed with the Williams and its Australian driver Alan Jones as new champions, and with the two most contentious issues of turbocharging and aerodynamic aids somewhat clarified.

When Renault first began to make headway with their turbocharged engine in Formula 1 racing, there had been attempts by jealous rivals to proscribe the turbocharger; but with this implement so firmly

The design of the Tyrell 6-wheeler was based on questionable premises, but the car occasionally went well. The power of advertising is evidently beyond question . . .

established in sports-car and other racing categories, thanks largely to the pioneering work of Porsche, the attempt was doomed to failure. Once it became clear that the engine formula was not to be altered, the attractions of the turbocharger were confirmed by a number of Renault's rivals. Ferrari had a turbocharged V6 ready by the end of the 1980 season, Alfa Romeo displayed a turbo V8 and promised a car to carry it, and the predominantly French combine lately renamed Talbot was expected to come into Grand Prix racing with a turbocharged car some time in 1981. There was even talk of Ford commissioning a new turbo engine from Cosworth or Zakspeed to keep happy all those whom the unboosted 3-litre V8 had served so famously for 13 years.

Arguments had been raging just as long about aerodynamic aids and appendages, but they became much more critical in 1978 when once again Colin Chapman took a substantial and scientific step ahead of his competitors. In that year the Italian-born American driver Mario Andretti – a very accomplished and unusually mature man in this milieu, having already reached the top of his profession in the USA – became world champion driver at the wheel of a Lotus that went almost unchallenged through the year. Chapman no longer relied on airfoils to generate negative lift that could force the car and thus its tyres more firmly into contact with the road: instead, the Lotus was pulled down by a suction generated beneath it. The underside of the car, or as much of it as possible on either side of the carefully narrowed central tub containing the driver and machinery, was shaped to form a venturi passage through which a large mass of air was guided from front to rear. The road surface itself formed one wall of the venturi, and the gap between it and the flanks of the car was sealed by moveable strips or fences that became known as skirts. As

Hot rods clash in the floodlit dust of a London suburban arena above left; a pneumatic wheelbrace readies the Renault for René Arnoux below; and above a turbocharged Lancia Monte Carlo leads a Porsche at Brands Hatch to clinch its 1979 Championship of Makes.

the rush of air through this passage was accelerated by the venturi contours, the air pressure under the car was significantly lowered: thus practically the entire plan area of the car could be used to generate downforce, rather than the much smaller area of the airfoils that regulations still permitted. With its tyres loaded so heavily (and yet weightlessly) the Lotus could outcorner and outbrake any car built according to previous conventions.

The idea was not entirely new, and once again the inspiration came from Chaparral. Nearly ten years earlier, the American firm had shaken the CanAm establishment out of their not particularly effulgent wits by fielding a car whose entire plan area, save only the front wheel arches, was skirted to form a plenum chamber underneath it, from which air was sucked out by a pair of fans driven by a separate small 2-stroke engine of 45 horsepower, such as might normally propel a snowmobile. Promptly and appropriately nicknamed the 'sucker car', this Chaparral 2J was driven by Jackie Stewart at its Watkins Glen debut in July 1970 when it made the fastest lap, and in subsequent CanAm races it was consistently the fastest car when driven by that formidable and still underrated English all-rounder Vic Elford. Acting on the notorious American principle of never giving a sucker an even break, the other competitors raised every imaginable object to the Chaparral, ranging from its supernumerary engine to the cloud of dust spread rearwards by those extractor fans; but the most telling objection, heavily emphasized by the erstwhile lawyer who ran the McLaren team in the USA, was that the car's fans and skirts contravened the earlier ban on moving aerodynamic surfaces. It was not the first time that a motor racing clique acted to forestall progress that

Venturi car: Andretti's Lotus 81 in the 1980 German GP. Note the airflow fences beneath the car.

might have upset their accepted order of things, nor would it be the last, when in December 1970 the FIA ruled that the Chaparral system was illegal.

This did not stop one Bernie Ecclestone from reintroducing it in a Formula 1 car in 1978. Ecclestone was as slight in diffidence as in stature, and might be noted among his other entrepeneurial achievements for being in control of the Brabham racing team and being chairman of FOCA, the Formula 1 Constructors Association. No doubt he enjoyed challenging the International Federation of Automobile Sport (FISA) when he entered for the 1978 Swedish Grand Prix a sucker-car which had the rare distinction that year of forcing Andretti to try so hard that his Lotus broke. The car was a Brabham, powered by an Alfa Romeo engine that presaged a more complete and fully-armed return to the fray by that famous Italian manufacturer; but a tailshaft from the transmission drove a rearward-facing fan which served exactly the same purpose as the fans at the rear of the Chaparral. In the Brabham, some of the air drawn from beneath the car was arranged to pass through the radiators, enabling Ecclestone blandly to dismiss the fan as part of the car's cooling system – but it was an argument that failed to impress anybody who had noted that when the Alfa Romeo engine was revved up the Brabham settled an inch nearer the ground. This took place at a time when the FISA and the FOCA were at the height of their mutual antagonism, and Ecclestone may have hoped to challenge the ruling body's authority; but he seems to have made an error of judgement, for the other constructors did not thank him for trying to pull a fast one as well over his friends as over his foes. The fan car was never raced again.

The venturi cars on the other hand grew more and more fantastic. The so-called 'kit car' manufacturers, the small specialist firms who relied on being able to buy a proprietary engine (invariably the Cosworth), were delighted, because the shape of this engine allowed plenty of space for air to be ducted through

The first venturi car, the Lotus 78, at the new Long Beach venue for the US Grand Prix West.

At the end of 1980 the fastest GP car yet, though not the most successful: the turbocharged 1½-litre Renault, driven here by Jean-Pierre Jabouille.

properly shaped passages. Admittedly there was a lot of tidying up that had to be done, with gearboxes, brakes, suspension and exhaust pipes being redesigned or rerouted to avoid interfering with the desired air flow, but that redesign was not such a great problem as was offered to Ferrari, Alfa Romeo and Renault by the shapes of their engines and ancillaries, which got in the way badly. Renault could do something in mitigation by shifting ducts and heat exchangers, but the two Italian firms could not do much about their wide low flat-12 engines which had so lately been sources of great power and pride. Alfa Romeo produced a V12 as quickly as possible for the chassis with which they finally made themselves respectable, making a car that was purely and wholly Alfa Romeo and occasionally quite competitive; Ferrari, as we have already seen, managed well enough in 1979 despite this handicap to secure the world championship, but by 1980 it was clear that they were in an even worse predicament than Renault, who had not been able to achieve a very effective venturi car; and it was probably this consideration as much as any other that prompted Ferrari to take the turbocharging course, since it was feasible for a purpose-built 1½-litre V6 to be as narrow as was appropriate to the needs of aerodynamics. On the other hand, Frank Williams' designer Patrick Head was able to shape a car so high in adhesion and so low in drag as to be often the fastest and throughout the 1980 season the most consistently fast of all contestants, winning the constructors' title for Williams as well as the world championship for Jones, and all with no more power than was available to any Cosworth customer.

The Tourist Trophy is run on a closed track now, not on real roads, but the right kind of car still wins. This BMW coupé won the 1980 TT.

If turbo-induced engine charging and aerodynamically-induced roadholding have together been the dominant features of Grand Prix racing since 1978 (as they have been, to the extent that certain drivers were heard to complain that the cars now mattered more than the drivers!) and if warfare between the competitors and the regulators has sometimes imperilled the future of either (skirts have been banned for 1981), all this technical and political activity in Formula 1 racing must be seen against a broad background of development and dissension throughout contemporary motor sport. Nowhere was this more evident than in the USA where, although they now entertain Formula 1 racers twice a year, the Americans otherwise remain staunchly isolationist in their principles and practices. They have there no single governing body, races being run under the auspices of a few large-scale organizations of which some are more professional than others, some more regional, and some more jealous or resentful of supposed rights and privileges. Rules and regulations vary according to the organizing 'club', loyalties are often intense, and tempers often inflamed. So impassioned did the feud become between two of the major clubs in 1980 that even the future of the celebrated 500-mile race at Indianapolis was put at hazard by their inability to reach any rapprochement. Meanwhile, if their native wit has not produced any new ideas since 1970, they have done some good engineering, and the latest form at Indianapolis is ample evidence to show that what works on one side of the Atlantic can work on the other. Practically all the most successful cars there are powered by turbocharged Cosworth engines, and the best of the venturi-effect cars – which, like the others, now regularly reach speeds of about 200 mph on the straights of the old circuit – can now be driven flat out all the way round the four corners as well. Success at Indianapolis is now not so much a matter of confidence in skills as of commitment to belief.

Elsewhere in America, while local traditions are properly respected, traditionally European values are not discounted, and most of Europe and probably the world was delighted when the 1979 Le Mans 24-hour sports-car race was won by a Porsche turbo coupé driven by a team of Americans. Their performance upset the form book considerably and in a most refreshing way for, although they were not the first American drivers to win that most important of races (after trying since the 1920s, success came in 1958 when the American Phil Hill shared the winning Ferrari with that patrician Belgian driver Olivier Gendebien), they were the first of them to be amateurs. Admittedly they were pretty wealthy amateurs, but this merely confirmed one of the earliest traditions of the sport while detracting not a whit from the respect due to their abilities.

Brainwashed and cowed though he may be by government agencies galore and social pressure groups operating at assorted levels of hypocrisy, the American motorist can still occasionally show a decently cloven hoof; and when he goes, it appears that he really goes, the law and profits notwithstanding. Every so often, and not more than once a year, a bunch of renegade leadfoots sets off in commemoration of that great transcontinental driver Cannonball Baker. Their object is simply to repeat his run 'from sea to shining sea' as quickly as possible and quicker than everybody else, facing every imaginable hazard of roads, traffic and police. Despite a nationwide speed limit of 55 mph, those who are able to do so maintain cruising speeds of 140 or more. Organized informally and unofficially by the well-known motor journalist Brock Yates, the race offers little or nothing in the way of prizes but a good deal in the way of penalties, and he is a fine fellow who wins it. A few years ago Brock travelled as co-driver with the celebrated all-round, all-American racer Dan Gurney in a Ferrari Daytona, and they only finished second, which gives some idea of how hectic the pace can be. The 1979 commemorative run was won by a Jaguar XKS from a 6.9 litre Mercedes Benz, and some of the vehicles with which they were competing were almost beyond belief. If this be the last of the great road-races, there is hope for the sport after all – but then, as it was said in the beginning, man cannot help being an idealist.

ENVOY

Tell me,
What is your opinion of Progress? Does it, for example,
Exist? Is there ever progression without retrogression?
Therefore is it not true that mankind
Can more justly be said increasingly to Gress?
As the material improves, the craftsmanship deteriorates,
And honour and virtue remain the same.

Christopher Fry

Back to the track for Pirelli? Backs to the wall for the kit-car manufacturers as the big names of the motor industry come back into racing? Back to reality, perhaps, as the demands of road and track merge, as the racers learn to use tyres that were cultivated for roadsters, and the road car profits from aerodynamics learned in racing. Specialization will probably intensify: for every convergence of technologies, there is a divergence of interests – and who knows what the public will want to see in the future? Economy trials?

Acknowledgements

The author and publishers gratefully wish to acknowledge the following for the use of their photographs. The numbers refer to the pages on which they appear.

(*colour*) All Sport 190, 194, 195, 214 Graham Gauld 160, 163, 167, 214 (below) Bruce Grant Braham 219 Louis Klemantaski 129 (above and below), 132, 133, 137 (above), 140, 141, 145 (above and below), 149, 152, 153, 156, 157, 171, 175, 178, 186, 187, 198 (*black and white*) Colin Taylor Productions 212 Graham Gauld 32 (above), 94 (below), 96/97, 114 (below), 147 (above), 173, 176, 183, 185 (above and below), 189 (above and below) Geoffrey Goddard 17, 20 (below), 31, 48 (above), 57, 60, 61, 74/75, 77 (above), 79 (above), 92 (above and below), 102, 105 (above and below), 111 (below), 117 (below), 119 (above and below), 120 (above and below), 121, 125 (below), 137 (below), 143 (above), 148 Cyril Posthumus 12/13, 15 (below), 16, 19, 20 (above), 23, 24/25, 26/27, 28, 29 (above and below), 33, 35, 38/39, 41 (below), 43, 44 (above), 45 (above and below), 48 (below), 49, 56, 58/59, 62, 62/63, 67 (below), 69, 71 (below), 73, 77 (below), 79 (below), 82 (below), 83, 85 (above and below), 86/87, 88 (above and below), 89, 90, 93, 95, 100/101, 106, 111 (above), 112 (above and below), 117 (above), 143 (below), 150, 155, 159 (above), 161, 169 (above)

Author's Collection (*colour*) 182, 191, 199 (above), 202 (above and below), 207, 211, 218 (*black and white*) 3, 4, 6, 15 (above), 22, 32 (below), 34, 36, 41 (above), 44 (below), 47 (above and below), 50/51, 64 (above and below), 67 (above), 68, 71 (above), 80, 82 (above), 94 (above), 98 (above and below), 107, 108, 109, 110, 113, 114 (above), 115, 122, 125 (above), 127, 128, 131 (above and below), 134, 135, 139, 144, 147 (below), 151, 158, 159 (below), 162, 164, 168, 169 (below), 172, 181, 192 (above and below), 196 (above and below), 197, 199 (below), 200, 201, 204 (above and below), 209, 210, 213, 215, 216, 217

Index

Numbers in *italic* type refer to illustrations

Aaltonen, Rauno, 191
Adler, 141
Alen, Marku, *210*
Alfa Romeo, 9, *82*, 95, 103, 109, 110, *111*, 121, 122, *122*, 123, 124, 126, 127, 128, 130, 133, *136*, 140, 141, 142, *142*, 144, *144*, 146, 148, 151, *151*, 154, *154*, 156, 157, 161, 174, 206, 212, 213, 216, 218
Alfetta, 139, 146, 154, 157
Allard, Sidney, 148, *149*
Alta, 141, *149*
Andretti, Mario, 205, 213, 216, *216*
Arnoux, René, *215*
Arrol-Johnston, 43
Ascari, Alberto, 144, 146, *158*
Ascari, Antonio, 144
Aston Martin, 36, 141, 153
Austin, *140*, *144*
Austin Healey, 168, *184*
Austro-Daimler, 46, *49*, *93*, 130, 180
Automobil Club von Deutschland, 34, 36
Automobile Association, 21
Automobile Club de France, 14, 18, 30, 65, 66, 70, 76
Auto-Union, 123, 124, 126, 130, *130*, 134, 138, 140, 144, 151, 162, 172, 180

Ballot, 80, 84, *88*, 89, 91, *91*
Barcelona, *126*
Barnato, Woolf, 104, 107
Barry, Sir James, 203
Bazzi, Luigi, 95
Beachey, Lincoln, 116
Becchia, 95
Bentley, 36, 103, 104, *104*, 107, *107*, 108, *108*, 109, *113*, 154
Bentley, Walter Owen, 104
Benjafield, Dr. Dudley, 104, 107
Benz, 17, 46, *46*, *68*, 91, *99*, 115, 179, 180, 181
Benz, Karl, *6*, 40
Beograd, 138, *138*
Berne, *136*
Bertarione, Vincenzo, 95
Berthon, Peter, 151
Bianchi, 91
Biondetti, Clemente, *112*, 148
Birkin, Sir Henry ('Tim'), 107, 108, 109, *113*
BMC (British Motor Corporation), *184*, 188, 190. *See also* Mini
BMW, 142, *142*, *219*
Bochet, Monsieur, 18
Bohringer, Eugen, *188*
Boillot, Georges, 70, 78, *80*
Bollée, 14, 16
Bonneville Salt Flats, 194
Bordino, Pietro, *51*, *83*, 121

Borghese, Prince Scipione, 7, 8
Bosch, 173
Brabham, 200, 216
Brabham, Sir Jack, 170, 172, 179, 181, 183, 198
Bradley, W. F., 99
Brands Hatch, *193*, *197*, *204*, *215*
Brauchitsch, Manfred von, 133, *134*
Breedlove, Craig, 195
Bremgarten, *144*
Brescia, 8, *36*, *37*, *65*, 109, 110
Brescia Automobile Club, 142
Bridgehampton, 197
Bristol, 179
Brivio, Marquis Antonio, 130
BRM, 151, 152, 158, 173, 187, 193, *200*
Brooklands, 46, *51*, 52, 56, 57, 60, 65, 83, *96*, 104, *110*, 141, *149*, 198, 203
Brooks, C. A. S. ('Tony'), 172, 173, 177, 179
Brovhot, 23
Bucharest, 142
Bugatti, 89, 91, *91*, 95, 99, *99*, 110, *111*, *112*, *113*, 121, 124, 126, 127, 128, *128*, 141, 144, 154
Buick, 57, 198
Burman, Bob, 116

Cabianca, Giulio, *169*
Caesar, Dick, *148*
Cagno, Alessandro, 65
Campari, Giuseppe, *82*, 121
Campbell, Donald, 195
Campbell, Sir Malcolm, 116
Canadian Automobile Sports Club, 195
Cappa, Giulio Cesare, 95
Caracciola, Rudolf, 104, 108, 109, *109*, 110, *118*, *126*, 130, 133, 151, 180
Carlsson, Erik, 188, *188*
Carrera Panamericana, *169*
Castellotti, Eugenio, *169*
Caters, Baron Pierre de, 10, 36
Cavalli, Carlo, 95
Chadwick, Lee, 95
Chaparral, 195, 197, *197*, 201, 215, 216
Chapman, Colin, 173, 183, 184, 193, 200, 209, 210, 213
Chasseloup-Laubat, Comte de, 17, 115
Chenard-Walcker, 103
Chevrolet, 10, 174
Chevrolet, Gaston, 80
Chevrolet, Louis, 80, 151
Chiron, Louis, *112*, 122, 133
Christie, *66*, 118
Christie, J. Walter, *66*
Chrysler, *107*, 194
Citröen, 188, 190
Clark, Jim, 10, *183*, 191, 193, *198*, 200, 201
Clarke, Thomas, *78*

Clement, Frank, 107, 108
Collins, Peter, *154*, 174, *174*
Connaught, 161, 170, 172
Cook, Humphrey, 140
Cooper, 161, *161*, 170, 172, 177, 181, 183, 184, 187, 188, 198. *See also* Mini-Cooper
Cooper, John, 179, 181
Costantini, Meo, *99*
Costin, Frank, 173
Costin, Mike, 200
Cosworth, *198*, 200, 203, 206, 211, 216, 220
Coventry Climax, 181, 187
Crystal Palace, *149*
CSI (Commission Sportive Internationale), 18

Daily Express, 152, 153
Daimler, *6*, 34, 35, 36, 180
Daimler-Benz, 124, *126*, 180, 181, *193*
Darracq, 19. *See also* Sunbeam-Talbot-Darracq and Talbot-Darracq
Davis, S. C. H. Sammy, 107, 108
Dawson, Joe, *56*
Daytona Beach, 116, *203*, 205
De Dietrich, 21, 23
De Dion, 11, 17, *116*, 118, 136, 138, 163
Delage, 91, 121, *133*, 139, 141, 144
Delahaye, 141, 144, 179
Delius, Ernst von, 136
DePalma, Ralph, 78, *88*, 89
Diatto, 91
Dieppe, *72*
Dion, Marquis de, 14
Dixon, Freddie, 118
Donington, 142
Dowson, George, *144*
Dreyfus, René, 130
Dubonnet, André, *99*
Duckworth, Keith, 200
Duesenberg, 84, 89, *89*, 91, 118
Dundrod, 166
Duray-Miller, 118
Durlacher, Cyril, *42*

East London, 198
Ebblewhite, A. V., 52
Eberhorst, Eberan von, 180
Ecclestone, Bernie, 216
Edge, S. F., 33
Edison, Thomas Alva, 95
Eldridge, Ernest, *96*
Elford, Vic, 215
Englebert, 173
ERA (English Racing Automobiles), *126*, 140, 146, *149*, 151

Fagioli, Luigi, 9, 133
Fangio, Juan Manuel, 9, *154*, 157, *158*, 161,

162, 166, 170, 173, 174
Farina, Dr. Giuseppe, 9, 138, 154
Farman, Henri, 19
Ferrari, *112*, 146, *146*, 151, 154, *154*, 156, 157, 158, *158*, 161, 162, *163*, 165, *169*, 170, 173, 174, *174*, 177, *177*, 181, 183, 184, 187, *187*, 188, 197, *197*, 198, *201*, *203*, 205, 206, 207, 208, 212, 213, 218, 220
Ferrari, Enzo, 144, 212
FIA, 216
Fiat, 36, 40, *46*, *51*, *52*, 65, *66*, 70, *70*, 72, 78, *82*, *83*, 91, *91*, 95, *95*, *96*, 118, 121, 136, 141, *141*, 144, *144*, 157, 161, 162, 172, 180, 206, 208, *208*, *210*, 211
Firestone, 191, 197
FISA (International Federation of Automobile Sport), 216
Fisher, Carl G., 56, 57, 80
Florio, Vincenzo, 65
FOCA (Formula I Constructors Association), 216
Ford, 148, 174, 191, *197*, 200, 203, *203*, 208, 211, *211*
Ford, Henry, 10
Fornaco, Guido, 95
Fournier, Henri, *21*
Frazer Nash, *84*, 141, 177
Frazer-Nash, Archie, *84*
Freikaiserwagen, *148*
Frontenac, 80, 89
Fry, Joe, *148*

Gabriel, Fernand, 23, 30, *68*
Gallop, Clive, *104*
Garot, Monsieur, 154
Gendebien, Oliver, 220
General Motors, 195, *197*
Georges Irat, 141
Giaconne, Signor, *93*
Giaur, 162
Giffard, Pierre, 14
Ginther, Ritchie, 197
GN, *84*
Gobron-Brillié, 157, *158*
Gonzales, Froilan, 157, *158*
Goodwood, *161*, 184
Goodyear, 191
Goossen, Leo, 118, 121
Gordini, *158*, 161, 165
Gordini, Amedée, 161
Gordon Bennett Cup, 30, *30*, 33, *33*, 34, 36, *40*, 42, 56, 66
Gordon Bennett, James, 30, 91
Goux, Jules, *88*
Grant, Gregor, *173*, *177*
Gregoire, *78*
Guinness, Algernon Lee, 179
Guinness, Kenelm Lee, 115, 179

Guizzardi, Ettore, 8
Gurney, Dan, 200

Hall, Jim, 195, 197
Hanstein, Baron Huschke von, 142
Harley-Davidson, 118
Hawthorne, Mike, 161, 166, 174, *174*
Head, Patrick, 218
Healey, Donald, 148
Heinrich, Prince, of Prussia, 46, *46, 49*
Hémery, Victor, 17, 115
Hemsley, Jack, 208
Henne, Ernst, 142
Henry, Ernest, 76, 78, 80, 89, 136
Herkomer, Herbert von, 46
Hieronymus, Otto, 36
Hill, Graham, 193
Hill, Phil, 188, 220
Hispano-Suiza, *99*
Hitler, Adolf, 124, 127, 180
Hockenheim, 201
Holden, Colonel Capel, 52
Honda, 200
Hopkirk, Paddy, 188, 190
Hotchkiss, *121*, 148, 154
Howmet, *198*
Hulme, Denny, *206*
Hunt, James, 205
Hus, Jan, 56

Indianapolis, 56, 57, 60, *60*, 78, *78*, 80, 83, 84, *88*, 89, *89*, 179, 187, 193, 203, 219, 220
Invicta, *118*, 148
Irimajiri, Shoichiro, 200
Isotta-Fraschini, *65*
Issigonis, Sir Alex, *144*
Itala, 7, 8, 65

Jabouille, Jean-Pierre, *218*
Jaguar, 153, 154, 166, *170*, 191
Jano, Vittorio, 95, 122, 170
Jarrott, Charles, 10, 21, 30, *33*
JAP, *161*
Jaussaud, Jean-Pierre, 207
Jellinek, Emile, 34, 35
Jenatzy, Camille, *30, 34*, 36, 37, 115
Jenkinson, Denis, 166
Johnson, Claude, *42*
Jones, Alan, 212, 218
Jörns, Carl, *84*

Keech, Ray, 116
Keene, Foxhall, 36
Kidston, Glenn, 107, 108
Kieft, *161*
Klementaski, Louis, *154*
Knyff, Chevalier René de, 9, 18, *68*

Lagonda, 141
Lampredi, Aurelio, 154
Lancia, *65*, 162, 165, 166, 170, 173, 208, *210*, *218*
Lancia-Ferrari, *158, 168*
Lancia, Vincenzo, *36*
Lang, Hermann, 133, *133*, 138, 151
Lauda, Niki, 205
Lautenschlager, Christian, *34*, 76, 78, *80*
L'Auto, 7, 8
Leopold, King, of Belgium, 40
Levassor, Emile, 14, *14*, 16, 30
Levegh, Pierre, 168
Lightweight Special, *144*
Livorno, 130
Locke-King, H. F., 52

Lockhart, Frank, 116, 121
Lola, 195
Long Beach, *217*
Lorraine-Dietrich, *68*
Lotus, *163*, 173, *177*, 183, *183*, 184, 187, *191*, 193, *193*, 197, *198*, *199*, 200, 201, 205, *206*, 209, 210, 213, 215, *216*
Lurani, Count Giovanni, 142

Macklin, Lance, 168
McLaren, 195, 203, 205, 206, *206*, 215
McLaren, Bruce, 181
Makinen, Timo, *184*, 190
Manx Rally, *211*
March, *204*
Marmon, *56*
Maserati, *118*, 124, 126, 127, 128, 139, 144, 146, 161, 162, 165, *165*, 170, 172, 173, 174, 198
Maserati brothers, 91
Masetti, Count Giulio, 10, *82, 93*
Massimino, Alberto, 95, 144
Matra, 203, 206, *206*
May, Michel, 197
Maybach, Wilhelm, 35, 40
Mays, Raymond, *118*, *126*, 140, 151, 152
Mercédès, 19, *21*, *30*, 34, *34*, 36, 37, 42, *60*, 72, 76, *76*, 78, 80, *80*, 82, 91, *93*, 95, 104, 108, 109, 110
Mercedes-Benz, 104, *108*, 109, *109*, 110, 118, 123, 126, *126*, 128, 130, *130*, 133, 134, *134*, 136, *136*, 138, *138*, 139, 144, 151, 156, 162, *162*, 163, *165*, 166, 168, *169*, 170, 177, 180, 206
Merkel, M., *16*
MG, 36, 108, 128, 141
Michelin, 207
Michelin, André, 14
Mille Miglia, 26, 86, 109, *109*, 110, 123, 140, *141*, 142, *144*, 148, *154*, 166, *169*, 170, *173*, 174, 177, *177*, 206
Miller, 89, *116*
Miller, Harry Armenius, 116, *116*, 118, 121
Milton, Thomas W., 80, 118
Mini (BMC), *184*, *187*, 188, 190, *190*
Mini-Cooper, 188, 190, 191
Minoia, Ferdinand, 65
Monaco, 110, *112*, 113, 166, *183*, 184, 201
Monroe-Frontenac. *See* Frontenac
Monte Carlo, 46, 49, 113, *115*, 115, 123, 148, 154, *184*, 188, *188*, 190, 191, *201*, 206, 208
Monza, 91, *93*, *95*, *111*, 146, *158*, 163, *165*, *174*, 180, 205
Mors, 9, 19, 21
Moss Stirling, 161, *161*, 165, *165*, 166, *172*, 173, 177, 179, 181, 184, 187, 193
Murphy, Jimmy, 118
Mussolini, Benito, 126, 127

Napier, 30, 33, 36, 76
NASCAR (National Association for Stock-Car Auto Racing), 194
Nazzaro, Felice, 65, 70, *70*
Neubauer, Alfred, 133, *134*, 139
Newman, Bob, 7, 8
New York Herald, The, 30
Niebel, Dr. Hans, 181
Northey, Percy, *42*, 43
Norton, 173
Nürburgring, 110, 128, *134*, 136, 140, 142, 165, *168*, 184, 197, 205
Nuvolari, Tazio, 110, *110*, 122, *122*, 123, 128, 130, 133, *134*, 138, 151

Offenhauser, 118
Oldfield, Barney, *34, 58*, 115, 118
Oliver, Eric, 166
Opel, *84*, 197
Osca, *169*
Owen, Hugh, 166

Packard, *35*, 84, 118
Paget, Hon. Dorothy, 104, 107
Panhard, 9, 14, 16, *16*, 18, 19, 33, 68, 188
Panhard-Levassor, *6*
Parker, Dorothy, 203
Parry, Thomas, J. G., 116
Pau, *113*
Pendine Sands, 117
Pescara, *158*, 172
Petit Journal, Le, 10, 14
Peugeot, *6*, 14, *70*, 72, 76, 78, 80, *80*, 84, 89, 104, 116, 141, 162
Pic-Pic, *78*
Pirelli, 7, 8, 83, 103, 128, 142, 144, *165*, 177, 208
Pironi, Didier, 207
Playa del Rey, 60
Pöge, H. Wilhelm, *34*
Polonez, 212
Poore, Denis, 151
Porsche, *93*, *146*, *166*, 177, 180, *188*, 191, 197, 206, 207, *215*, 220
Porsche, Ferdinand, 46, 180, 181
Portago, Marquis de, 170, *177*
Porter, 23
Premier, 80
Prescott, *126*, *144*, *151*
Prudhomme, Don, 194

Rabe, Karl, 180
RAC (Royal Automobile Club), 33, 42, 83, 208
RAC Rally, *184*, *188*, *191*, 210
Ramponi, Giulio, 107, 108
Reims, *152*, 163
Renault, *23*, 26, 66, 70, 148, 207, 208, 211, 212, *213*, *215*, 218, *218*
Renault, Louis, 19, *23*, 26, 30
Renault, Marcel, 19, 23, *23*, 29, 30
Resta, Dario, 80
Richard-Brasier, 37, *40*
Rigolly, Louis, 115
Riley, 140, 161
Rindt, Jochen, 205, *206*
Rochet-Schneider, 16
Roger-Benz, *6*, *13*
Rolland-Pilain, 91
Rolls, Hon. Charles S., 42, *42*, 43
Rolls-Royce, 42, *42*, *44*, 46, 173
Rosemeyer, Bernd, 130, 134, 138
Rosenberger, Adolf, 180
Rougier, Henri, 113
Royce, F. H., Ltd, 42
Royce, Sir Frederick Henry, 42, 43
Rumpler, Doktor, 180, 181

Saab, 188, *188*
Salzer, Otto, *44*
San Sebastian, *99*, *112*
Scales, Jack, *78*
Scarfiotti, Lodovico, 201
Scheckter, Jody, 207
Schiller, 205
Schlesser, Jo, 201
Seaman, Richard, 138, 139, 179
Sebastian, 110

Segrave, Sir Henry, 116, 172, 179
Sharp, Hap, 195
Shelsley Walsh, 40, 42, *118*, 123, 130, 151
Silverstone, 152, 153, 157, *162*, 165, 179, *200*, 206
Simca, 161
Spa-Francorchamps, *180*, *197*
Spence, Mike, 201
Stead, 23
Stewart, Jackie, 10, 203, 206, *206*, 215
Straight, Whitney, *118*
Straker-Squire, *49*
Strang, Lewis, 57
Strasbourg, 91, *91*
Stuck, Hans, 130, *130*
Stutz, *107*, 116
Sunbeam, *49*, *72*, 95, 115, 172
Sunbeam-Talbot-Darracq, 91
Syracuse, 172
Szisz, Ferenc, 70, 72

Tadini, Mario, *122*, 140
Talbot, *112*, 144, 146, 213. *See also* Talbot-Darracq and Sunbeam-Talbot-Darracq
Talbot-Darracq, 121. *See also* Sunbeam-Talbot-Darracq
Taraschi, Bernardo, 162
Targa Florio, 60, *60*, 65, *65*, 72, *82*, 83, *88*, *93*, 95, 99, *99*, 128, 140, 141, 144, 146, 166, 177
Taruffi, Piero, *177*
The Motor, *52*, *56*
Théry, Leon, 37
Thistlewaite, 'Scrap', *104*
Tourand, 23
Trevoux, Jean, 148, 154
Tripoli, 139
Triumph, 141
Trossi, Count Carlo Felice, 151
Turcat-Méry, *49*, 113
Tyrrell, 205, *213*

Uhlenhaut, Rudolf, 136, 165

Vanderbilt Cup, *44*, *57*
Vanderbilt, Mrs W. K., *44*
Vandervell, Anthony, 173
Vanwall, 170, *172*, 173, 174, 177, 183
Varzi, Achille, 122, 128, 151
Vauthier, *29*
Vauxhall, 46, *49*, *88*
Vélocipéde, Le, 11
Ventoux, Mont, *118*
Villoresi, Luigi, 144
Voisin, *95*

Wagner, Louis, 181
Walker, Rob, 179
Watkins Glen, 215
Werner, Wilhelm, 35, 104
Wharton, Ken, 148
White-Triplex, 116
Wilhelm II, Kaiser, 37
Williams, 212, 218
Wimille, Jean-Pierre, 151
Wolseley, *33*

Zakspeed, 213
Zandvoort, *183*, 200
Zborowski, Count Eliot, 19
Zehender, Geofredo, 133
Zerbi, Tranquillo, 95
Zuylen de Nyefelt, Baron, 14